GOD'S CRUCIBLE

WE WHO DREAM OF A BETTER LIFE

Stories of Hope by Refugee and Immigrant Youth

BY
CUONG QUY HUYNH

aBM

Published by:

A Book's Mind

PO Box 272847

Fort Collins, CO 80527

Copyright © 2019

Edited by: Peggy Scolaro

ISBN: 978-1-949563-57-3

Printed in the United States of America

Cru·ci·ble - /ˈkroosəb(ə)l/ [noun] - a situation of severe trial, or in which different elements interact, leading to the creation of something new. (Source: Oxford Dictionary at Lexico.com)

PRAISE FOR GOD'S CRUCIBLE

"Cuong Quy Huynh's book, *God's Crucible: We Who Dream of a Better Life*, is not only a story describing the personal hopes of immigrants and refugees. This book is truly a story of how America has become a great country and how it can continue to grow into becoming even a greater country.

Cuong's personal story and the stories of other immigrant youths who are now and will become influential leaders of our future, should give all of us hope and inspiration.

God's Crucible:We Who Dream of a Better Life, is a must read for all of us who are committed to "Be the change we want to see in others" (a quote from Mahatma Gandhi)."

—Bing Goei, Successful Immigrant Entrepreneur
CEO of Eastern Floral Company and the Goei Center, Grand Rapids, Michigan

"Cuong Huynh is a living example of one whose life story calls others to excellence. Turning difficulties into opportunities, he now inspires others. *God's Crucible: We Who Dream of a Better Life* makes it clear that life can be a great adventure filled with meaning."

—Bill Shuler, Lead Pastor, Capital Life Church

"Mr. Huynh has pulled together powerful stories of courage, resilience and hope. These are the traits that imbue the American spirit and which continue to strengthen our nation. We can all learn from some of our newest citizens and be reminded of why we love our country so much."
—Ambassador Gina Abercrombie-Winstanley

"Cuong's story is a remarkable and transformative journey. You'll find yourself drawn into his journey - the ins-and-outs and ups-and-downs - a crucible that shaped him to be a man that continues to make a difference in the lives of many others. Walking alongside of him over the last decade, I enjoy the qualities of hope, joy, faithfulness, determination and integrity that resonates both in and through his life. I commend not only this book, but his life, to you!"
—Dave Buehring, Founder & President, Lionshare Leadership Group

CONTENTS

ACKNOWLEDGEMENTS

This book is dedicated to refugee and immigrant youth and their families, especially those coming from low-wealth backgrounds and households, living now in the United States of America.

As I complete writing this book, I want to acknowledge my mentors and friends in my life who have made writing this book possible: Bill Halamandaris, Virginia Chavez, Tom McCandless, Dave Buehring, Bill Shuler, Lisa Shuler, J.C. Lowery, Ambassador Gina Winstanley, Ambassador Edward Perkins, John Lee, Willis Jenkins, Bill Dombi, Val Halamandaris, Janeane Vigliotti, Bing Goei, Maria Manetta, Tom Rowe, Chris O'Neal, Peggy Scolaro, and Colleen Noland.

Further, I want to thank my parents, Anh Duong and Phat Huynh, and my siblings: Helen, Lana, Lanie, Eric, Jimmy, Victor, Donn, Jennifer, and Roger, for taking the huge risks of leaving Vietnam to flee to a different country that promised political and economic freedom. My parents and siblings have taught me the importance of this truth: Family comes first. We are very grateful to be here together in the United States. We are living our dreams of better lives in America.

Additionally, I want to thank the immigrant and refugee youth mentioned in this book for sharing their stories with me. Their stories have helped me to see the enormous potential of this nation to do so much more and to build a more perfect union -— to be a more inclusive American society by providing opportunities for immigrants and refugees who come to the United States and to set positive role models for all of us.

Also, I want to thank my wife, Jesecca, and my daughter, Lucie Mei, for showing me unconditional love and selflessness while writing my book.

Essentially, I want to thank our God – Jesus Christ. He has shown me that we are all spiritual immigrants, and He is the source of everything in my life and in my family. We are deeply grateful to God for bringing my family and me to America and for giving us a new future as new Americans in the wonderful nation called the United States of America.

FOREWORD

This is a book *for* refugee and immigrant youth and their families in the United States, written *by* refugee and immigrant youth.

It is their story, but it also our story. We are all – with few exceptions – immigrants or the descendants of immigrants.

For more than 500 years, people from all over the world have made their way to America. We have become, in the words of Israel Zangwill, "God's Crucible," the great melting pot where all the races are converging and reforming.

Some now question this tradition. They feel immigrants place an unacceptable burden on society, but the simple fact is that the rich and powerful are satisfied with their lot and do not leave it. The promise of America is for the rest of us: we who dream of a better life.

In seeking to advance themselves, immigrants advance our nation. But few have come as far so fast as Cuong Huynh, the inspiration and author of this book. I met Cuong in 1990 when I helped honor him with a National Caring Award and marvel since he received that recognition just eleven years after arriving in the United States.

My family and most of my friends are children of immigrants. Each has his or her own story. Each has lived the American Dream, but few can match the determination and reliance shown by the courageous people whose stories follow. They remind us what America is all about.

Bill Halamandaris
Co-founder, Heart of America Foundation

PREFACE

uong Huynh was born in Vietnam and had lived in two refugee camps in Malaysia by the age of six. He knew extreme poverty as a refugee and continued to live in deprivation in his early years after settling in the United States. However, Cuong did not let his destitute experiences define him. His optimism has not changed from the young volunteer student I met in the early 1980s to the present day. His zest to give back to the world and community has never wavered through the years I have known him.

I have been in the volunteer management and leadership-training arena for over twenty-five years, mentoring youth volunteers and assisting them in achieving their higher education goals. As a mentor, it has been a gift to see the results of my efforts transformed in Cuong as he has superseded my support. Cuong's life demonstrates the results of positive youth development guidance. He carried the lessons he learned in early leadership programs and founded a nonprofit organization, the Enlightened Initiative, which supports immigrant and refugee youth, especially those coming from low-wealth backgrounds.

Many of the stories contained in this book are about the immigrant and refugee youth he served as a mentor. Their "coming to America" stories share some similarities to Cuong's journey: some overcame language barriers, extreme poverty, and discrimination, and others had parents who struggled to gift their children with the benefits of this great nation. We are a nation of immigrants, and how we mentor youth and support them will define us as a country.

Virginia Nonaca Chavez

Co-founder, Leadership Concepts, Inc.

INTRODUCTION

A few of my professional and life mentors and friends have asked me, "Why have you not written a book about your refugee experience of leaving Vietnam, staying in refugee camps in Malaysia, plus growing up in poverty in your early years after settling in the United States?"

The answer is simple. I was not ready to tell my story until the year 2019. After completing a summer leadership camp for the immigrant and refugee youth in 2018, one of my mentors asked me again, "When are you writing your book?"

I said "soon" in a respectful way to my mentor.

The "soon" became a reality in 2019 because my family and I have lived in the United States for *40* years since arriving in 1979. Hence, I have written a book about my life from leaving Vietnam, staying in two refugee camps in Malaysia, growing up in poverty, and living on welfare and food stamps in my public-school years until I went to the University of California, Los Angeles (UCLA) at age 18.

My story and other immigrant and refugee youth's stories are written to let other vulnerable youth and their families living in the United States know that we understand the difficult obstacles and struggles they face. Yet, with the support of families, friends, mentors, coaches, community counselors, and God, we have overcome the difficult struggles and hardships of leaving our native countries and adjusting to life in America. By overcoming grueling trials as refugee and immigrant youth in the United States, the youth and I have been through God's crucible to become who we are today.

I hope that educators, counselors, non-profit organizations, companies, teachers, administrators, mentors, and other professionals who work with and encounter vulnerable youth daily will read this book to obtain a better and more comprehensive understanding of the lives of the youth in America.

It is with cultural sensitivity and understanding of the youth that this book aims to educate and share with the American public and this wonderful nation.

I hope you will see the amazing, resilient, and empowering qualities that these immigrant and refugee youth bring to this country, both now and in the future. These are young immigrants and refugees who, with their families, have overcome many fierce trials in their dream of finding a better life in America. Similar to me, these youth have passed through God's crucible of many difficult trials in leaving their native countries and resettling into the United States to help support their families and to serve their communities.

PART I
MY REFUGEE STORY

CHAPTER 1
LEAVING VIETNAM

" Wake up, wake up," called my mother, Anh Duong. It was in the middle of the night around two a.m. on a weekday, and I asked, "Where are we going?"

My mother said, "We are leaving!"

"Where?" I asked.

"We must leave our home," she replied. "We are going somewhere else." Not wanting to displease my mother and not knowing the next moves, I followed her instructions. Quickly, I put on my clothes and followed my mother out of the house in Saigon, renamed Ho Chi Minh City, in Vietnam. There I was with my parents and older siblings, ready to ride on the motorized rickshaws to go to a nearby harbor to leave Vietnam in 1978.

Later that morning, I learned that my family and I were leaving Vietnam permanently because of the rise of the communist Vietnamese government and other reasons, as well. I was excited to go with my family, but I was not sure where we were going. I knew that all I wanted to do was to follow my family.

I was born in Saigon on August 21, 1972, during the Vietnam War, and I am the youngest of 10 living children in my family. The Vietnam War had begun on November 1, 1955, and it ended on April 30, 1975. The Vietnam War occurred because there was a major conflict between the United States and the communist Vietnamese government. After France withdrew its troops from Vietnam, the United States feared that, under the Geneva Accords, there would not be free and fair elections for both North and South Vietnam. Also, the United States was very concerned with the presence of communism in the nation of Vietnam. The United States feared that the doctrine of communism could spread throughout Southeast Asia and thus become a greater political and economic threat to America.

Nevertheless, after years of unsuccessful fighting and enormous American casualties, on April 30, 1975, as South Vietnam began to collapse in the face of a North Vietnamese surge into the country, the United States withdrew from Vietnam. My family and I continued to live in the now communist state. Under communism in Vietnam, our family did not have freedom, nor did we have private property rights. For example, a police officer could have come into my family's household and taken whatever he wanted. He would just proclaim that item as a property of the communist government. Hence, my family and I did not even have private property rights in our own home.

Once the Vietnam War ended in April 1975, my family stayed in Vietnam because my grandfather, Duc Huynh, and father, Phat Huynh, had a dental practice. At that time, they still could earn enough to feed our family members. We had a large extended family. My grandfather, grandmother, and my parents had to take care of at least 10 children.

We were very fortunate to have enough income and resources to survive, such as material items and food, given that we were living in the communist government and that there were so many members of our family. My older siblings took care of me, and my parents worked very hard to provide for all my siblings and me. We were lucky to still have a big house at that time.

Nonetheless, living in Saigon under the communist rule became intolerable for my family after 1975. We did not have the freedom of having personal property rights, and we were also suspects by the new ruling communist government.

Additionally, the communist government wanted to punish those who had been their adversaries during the war. These adversaries included South Vietnamese soldiers who had sided with the United States or their allies, those of ethnic Chinese descent. The government sought to take away their real estate and/or personal property. The communist government did not like the ethnic Chinese residents because the government thought of the Chinese people as security threats against the Vietnamese government.

My family and I were among the ethnic Chinese Vietnamese in the country. At that time, in the 1970s, the Chinese and the Vietnamese governments were in a war with each other. The ethnic Chinese controlled most of the retail trade in South Vietnam, and the Vietnamese government did not like the fact that the Chinese had a stronghold in the retail business. The Vietnamese government restricted business activities, levied high taxes, and took over businesses owned by ethnic Chinese in South Vietnam.

Perhaps most frightening for my family, especially for my parents, was the fact that I had five older brothers (Eric, Jimmy, Victor, Donn, and Roger), who, due to the country's mandatory conscription, could have been forced to serve in the Vietnamese military. My parents were not prepared to sacrifice their sons in the military conflicts in Southeast Asia such as the war between China and Vietnam.

Because of the communist government and the mandatory conscription of my older brothers, my parents decided to leave Vietnam in 1978. They left with hopes of a better future outside their homeland. My family was among over one million Vietnamese and ethnic Chinese residents who risked their lives by traveling on crowded boats to flee from the place we called home. We fled to countries around the

South China Sea to other Southeast Asian countries such as Indonesia, Malaysia, Thailand, Philippines, Singapore, and to Hong Kong.

My grandparents, parents, siblings, and I had to make a clandestine departure from Vietnam. So, around two o'clock in the morning on a weekday in the summer of 1978, my family and I left our home in motorized rickshaws and hurried to a nearby harbor. There, a fishing boat was waiting, filled with others eager to escape from Vietnam. At Rach Gia Harbor, my grandparents, parents, older siblings, and I climbed into the boat, leaving our country in the hopes of a better future.

The fishing boat had two levels. The top level was filled with less healthy adults and vulnerable elderly, the disabled, and younger children. The bottom level was filled with healthy adults who were more likely to endure and tolerate a long trip on the treacherous open sea. Almost all of us were scared to leave Vietnam, but we wanted to leave our native country for better socio-economic and political futures. The refugees on the boat were mainly from lower-middle-class backgrounds that could afford to pay to be in a fishing boat in order to leave the country.

My family and I were on the fishing boat for over three days. For me, it felt like over a week. The roiling sea nauseated me, making me throw up what little I could eat. That unfamiliar place confused me, and my mother tried to comfort me and feed me familiar shredded pork she had packed for meals on the first part of our trip. However, I was too upset to eat. I was not even hungry, and what I did eat would not stay down in my stomach; I threw it all up. The rough open sea just took away my appetite. I was fortunate to not die in the open sea.

From among the thousands of Vietnamese leaving the country, it has been estimated that over 300,000 individuals died in the open sea trying to escape. Pirate ships from Thailand and other Southeast countries sank some boats, would rob the refugees and immigrants by taking their valuables jewelry, gold, diamonds, and leave the boats adrift for over several weeks with no food or water for the refugees to survive.

Vulnerable refugees, or the "boat people," as many people called us, encountered severe storms, unhealthy and unsanitary conditions, thirst, sickness and diseases, hunger and starvation, and had to also seek ways to avoid the dangerous pirates lurking on those open sea waters.

The refugees in my family's fishing boat were very lucky. We did not encounter hostile pirates, nor face stormy, dangerous weather that could have sunk our boat. Although we had barely enough food to eat to survive the open sea, fortunately, we had water to drink to ward of dying of thirst during the sea journey.

One of my brothers, Roger, said, "God is with us." Indeed, God was with us, although I did not know about Him at that time. Similarly, my mother said, "We were very lucky to survive the open sea without any major incidents such as robbery by pirates and stories of cannibalism in our fishing boat."

Instead, on the last day of our three days in the open sea, an unexpected and a powerful storm pushed our fishing boat deep into the shores of Malaysia. There, because of the strong wind driving our boat so forcefully, the local Malaysian authorities were unable to compel the fishing boat back out to the open sea. The fishing boat was literally stuck in the shores because of the strong winds and waves. The Malaysian authorities did not want more Vietnamese refugees coming to their land, especially those like my family, who are of ethnic Chinese descent.

Generally, back then, the Malaysian people, some with radical Muslim backgrounds, did not like the pork-eating Chinese Vietnamese. Fortunately, despite our heritage, all the refugees in our fishing boat were allowed to stay on the shores of Malaysia.

My family and I were very fortunate to survive the open sea journey. We could have been dead, and literally, we were playing "Russian roulette" with our lives without knowing how we would survive the open sea journey once we left Vietnam. Indeed, God was with us leaving Vietnam, and God was with us during the open sea journey. Further, God created powerful storms and winds to push our fishing boat deeply into the shores of Malaysia, so we could land in that country.

CHAPTER 2
REFUGEE EXPERIENCE

Once the fishing boat was stuck in the beach of Malaysia, I remembered jumping off and onto the shore. Fortunately, one of my brothers, Victor, caught me. The Malaysian authorities told us to set up a camp close to a beach shore. It was about two days before my grandparents, parents, older siblings, and I got to the nearby shelter where the Malaysian government processed refugees from Vietnam. The Malaysian authorities registered us as refugees after we set up our campsite.

My family stayed in the section of the country the Malaysian authorities set aside for the thousands of Vietnamese refugees. Many were in transit to other countries in Southeast Asia. Some refugees were on their way to Hong Kong, still under British rule, and others to places like Indonesia, the Philippines, Singapore, and Thailand.

My family and I stayed at least 11 months in two different refugee camps in Malaysia. It was a very difficult, trying experience for us. My father was often sick in the camps, as were many other refugees who suffered from asthma, tuberculosis, excessive coughs, malaria, and mental health issues. I recalled hearing my father's coughs so often at night that I thought he might die in Malaysia. He was not healthy while we stayed in the two refugee camps and often visited the nearby medical clinic in the camps. He barely received adequate medicines to assist with his coughs. However, my father was grateful to receive any medicine at all given that all of us were refugees. As refugees, my family and I had no legal status, and no country wanted us, including our native country of Vietnam.

Refugees also suffered from mental stress. The mental anguish took its toll on the refugees; some lost their sanity, succumbing to various mental illnesses. For example, one father of a different family who was living close to us in the refugee camp would walk around talking non-stop about matters unrelated to our living conditions and appeared to be mentally unstable. This man's clothing was disheveled, and he kept on muttering words non-stop, without making any coherent sense in normal conversations. As refugees, we were so vulnerable and were "disposable" people. No one would care for the refugees because we had no legal status from any nation.

My family and I were used to being in control, and we had been able to take care of the family back in Vietnam, especially before the communist government takeover. However, in the two Malaysian refugee camps, we learned what it feels like to be hungry, poor, and powerless. Having little choice regarding our lives and fate, we were forced into passivity. Yes, the United National Children's Fund (UNICEF) brought in food and water, but it was a long wait between shipments. With the help from UNICEF and other refugee aid organizations, food and water had to be brought in by barge and other boat shipments. Water was rationed generally to one gallon per person in each refugee camp. Hence, the refugees always felt desperation, and we always felt very vulnerable and hopeless.

The food we were given consisted of mainly canned sardines or tuna, rice, and vegetables. One of my older brothers, Donn, had the responsibility for our food rations. He had to be very alert, planning carefully, so we would have enough food and water to last until the next UNICEF shipment would arrive. We were just surviving day-by-day, week-by-week. We were simply very disenfranchised and marginalized. Refugees have no protection from any nation. If we were to die, no country would claim our bodies or would even care about who we were.

To survive in the refugee camps, for example, during a week, my older brothers would go to nearby forests to cut trees to have wood, so we could cook our food and have warmth to survive the cold during the evening times. Thanks to my older brothers, we did not have to worry about getting sick from eating raw and undercooked food. My grandfather encouraged my older brothers to find wood, so we could survive. I once saw them bringing back over 40 pounds of wood for us to cook with. My mother would use the wood to cook the canned foods and vegetable soups from UNICEF and other aid organizations for my grandparents, my father, my siblings, and me.

My mother is a heroine. Knowing that I might be sick from the unhealthy conditions in the refugee camps, she would heat up cold water for me to take a warm shower, so I would not get sick from pneumonia, given I was only six years old. She would cook all day, since there were at least over nine individuals living in our campsite. Sometimes, my mother would share our food with our surrounding neighbors who barely had enough to eat. We were simply surviving. What I saw in my mother's activities to help her family were examples of a servant leader. She worked hard to make sure everyone in our family was eating. To this day, I do not think my family would have survived without my mother's hard work cooking for the whole family.

With the forest trees, plastic sheeting, and using flattened tin cans from the used canned food, my grandfather, my father, and my older siblings built a shelter for our family. That tin floor in our campsite helped us to survive and not get too cold at nighttime and not get sun-burned in the daytime. Plus, the tin floor prevented the sands coming from the winds to get into our food; thus, we were able to eat without having sand in our mouths.

The refugee camps were lonely and dreadful places. We felt isolated and alienated. We had few genuine friends and no contact with the Malaysian government. We felt helpless, and we were unsure of how we would gain contacts that could aid us in getting out of the refugee camps. We were very vulnerable and marginalized.

Unsanitary conditions in the refugee camps led to negative health issues. There were no effective medicines to help my father with his incessant coughing. I suffered from bug bites because of mosquitos, often itching and scratching for days. I had scars on both my legs and arms because of the unsanitary conditions and the bug bites from mosquitos. Because I was a young refugee, I could not get the necessary medical skin cream to take care of my bug bites and skin scars.

Most difficult for many of us in the refugee camps was the absence of sanitized and decent bathrooms or toilets to use. Malaysian authorities would dig holes about 30 feet wide and 20 feet deep for refugees to use for urinating and passing bowels. Filled with fecal matter and other bodily fluids, the giant hole was simply filthy, muddy (especially in the rainy season), smelly, and completely unsanitary for any human being to use. One day, to my horror, I accidentally dropped my walking sandal in the deep hole. Because I had no other shoe to wear, I asked one of my older brothers, Victor, to pick up the dropped sandal from the deep hole.

Victor asked me, "What happened to your sandal?"

I replied, "I dropped one of my sandals in the urinating and bowels deep hole. Can you get it for me?"

Victor exclaimed, "NO WAY! There is no way that I am going to get your sandal out of that deep smelly and dirty hole. You can get it yourself."

I said, "I am too young to know what to do. You are older. You need to help me."

Victor looked at me and shook his head sideways. Then, he said, "OK, this time only. Next time, we are going to throw away that sandal."

Later, he took a long stick from the nearby forest to pick up my sandal from the filthy deep hole. Victor helped me because I was his younger brother, but he regretted having to pick up the sandal because it was simply so smelly, disgusting, and completely filthy. Fortunately, Victor also washed the sandal for me. He was really nice to do that for me.

Furthermore, the giant hole was dangerous because anyone (especially a child under five years old) could have fallen inside and drowned in the fecal matter and other bodily fluids. In that sense, the refugees were treated like animals. One could smell the unsanitary stench from the deep filthy hole over 400 feet away!

In these desperate refugee living conditions, my family and I waited for interviews with a United States immigration representative and hoped an American citizen would sponsor us. How elated we were to learn that after staying over 11 months in Malaysia, an uncle in the United States finally managed to work through the American immigration bureaucracy and complete the paperwork to sponsor us. We were more than ready to get out of the grim and filthy living conditions in the refugee camps, so far from home and filled with such uncertainty.

Years later, reflecting on my life in those two refugee camps, I promised myself that if I were to have a chance to help other children and families with issues of poverty, hopelessness, disenfranchisement, and marginalization, I would do so without hesitation.

I know from personal experience how difficult and challenging it was to live in such extreme destitution as a refugee in Malaysia. While there, I had no future goals other than staying alive long enough to leave. I was simply living day by day. I had no hope of getting an education or having a family of my own. However, once I was no longer living in such despicable and filthy refugee conditions in Malaysia, I realized that my refugee experience significantly marked my life. As I matured, I recognized it was my privilege and responsibility to invest in other people, especially children and youth, to assist them in reaching their dreams and goals as I had been able to do, once my family reached a safer place to live.

CHAPTER 3

EARLY YEARS SETTLING IN
THE UNITED STATES

In September 1979, my family and I left the refugee camps of Malaysia to travel to the airport. There, airplanes were on hand to fly refugees to the countries of accepting families of refugees. The United States and other western countries such as Canada, Australia, Sweden, and Britain, sponsored refugees from Southeast Asia, including Malaysia. I was so excited to leave the refugee camps!

Entering the Pan American Airways airplane was my first experience of even sitting on an airplane seat, much less flying. I told myself on the airplane that I was finally leaving the horrible refugee place where there was no future and no sanitized living conditions. I was going somewhere where I hoped I would not have to scratch my legs and arms any further from the bug bites from mosquitos. How lucky I felt to be leaving the deplorable living conditions. I felt relieved and very grateful to leave the negative and filthy living conditions in the refugee camps and go to a different country. No more waiting for UNICEF canned goods. No more living in tin shelters. No more going to the toilet in putrid and filthy outdoor pits. No more bug bites from mosquitos with nothing to ease the itching in the unsanitary, unhealthy refugee camps.

Once we landed in the Los Angeles International Airport (LAX) in the latter part of September 1979, one of my father's relatives picked us up. My father knew him from his days in Vietnam, and they were related as distant cousins. Our family stayed in his house for several days until we found our own rental apartment in the City of Los Angeles, California.

Our new home was a one-bedroom apartment in an old apartment complex near downtown Los Angeles. My family and I were living in a low-income neighborhood called "the barrio." I went to a public elementary school where I enrolled in English as a Second Language (ESL) classes. I started in the second grade, and I learned the basics of English.

While living in this low-wealth community, one time my family's small apartment got robbed, and some of our valuables were stolen from us. Our beds and the furniture were overturned because the robbers wanted to find the valuables in our apartment. The robbers took our money and some household items. My family and I felt violated, and we again felt isolated and hopeless because we could not report the robbery to the police department given our limited English verbal abilities. My parents and I did not know English well, and we felt we had to rebuild ourselves again after the robbery incident because we had to rely only on ourselves.

Our apartment had a small kitchen and a small bathroom. We had been unable to bring anything with us from Vietnam because we were refugees fleeing our native country, and we were impoverished. My parents slept in the bedroom, and my four older siblings and I shared the living room. My sister, Jennifer, had the couch to herself while my older brothers and I slept on one queen-size bed in the living room. I used to wear my older brothers' "hand-me-down" clothes because my parents could not afford new clothes for me to wear. Even as a seven-year-old boy, I realized that my family and I were struggling financially to make ends meet.

The English language was a barrier for us. Though my father was a dentist in Vietnam, neither he nor my mother could speak English very well. They could not find good paying jobs once we settled in Los Angeles. However, my older siblings worked different part-time jobs to provide food, clothing, and shelter for the family. Two of my older brothers, Victor and Donn, worked as waiters in a Chinese restaurant in Chinatown located close to the City of Los Angeles to get additional income to pay our rent and other living expenses. The restaurant owners knew that my brothers were vulnerable and marginalized due to their limited English knowledge and speaking abilities and needed the jobs to survive in America. Back then, in the early 1980s, Victor and Donn received below minimum wages of less than $5.00 per hour because they could not yet speak English very well. Donn said, "The restaurant managers know that we can not speak English very well, and we cannot fight back. So, the managers take advantage of us by not giving us all the tips from the customers who eat at the Chinese restaurant."

Along with Victor's and Donn's stories, I heard of other stories of exploitation against immigrants and refugees because they did not understand the American cultural norms, the language, and the laws and regulations of the United States. That is, refugees and immigrants worked in low-wage jobs just to survive because of the discrimination and bias against them in the American labor market.

My other older siblings, Eric and Jimmy, went to a high school and a technical college to learn vocational skills. They worked in low-paying jobs just to survive. We became humble, having to live modestly, surviving from month to month, because we arrived penniless as refugees from Malaysia.

We did learn through the Vietnamese community-based organizations that, as impoverished refugees from Vietnam, we were eligible for federal and state government assistance. My parents received food stamps, assisted housing vouchers, and welfare to help feed our family, pay rent, and buy other necessities to survive in America. Although my parents received the governments' assistance, they were required to go to school, learn English, and to learn a vocational skill to seek employment. The federal and state governments wanted my parents to eventually wean themselves off the governments' food stamps and welfare and to become self-sufficient.

As a seven-year-old, I went to second grade in a public elementary school in Los Angeles County. As a new refugee to the United States, I had to learn English and had to take "English as a Second Language" courses. The teachers would encourage me to say different words in English such as "safety pin," "books," "pencils," "clothes," and "backpacks" to build my English vocabulary and knowledge. The learning process was very interesting to me because I did not learn about any academic English subjects when I was a refugee in Malaysia. I came to the United States in September 1979 with few English vocabulary words to fully integrate into the American society.

I began adjusting to our new home in America. School was fun for me. I liked to play games during the school recess with my classmates. I also enjoyed being at home because my parents made sure that we had food to eat and sufficient clothes to wear. I relished spending time with my ten-year-old brother, Roger, back then. We would go out fishing at Echo Park in Los Angeles, where we hung out just enjoying each other's company. On many Saturday mornings, Roger and I would take our fishing poles to catch fish to bring back to our mother, so she could cook the fish for the whole family. Usually, we would catch about four or five middle-size fish to bring home. I thought Roger and I were being providers for the family since we caught fish for my family members to eat.

During those years of limited financial resources, my mother learned to shop scrupulously with food stamps. She made sure we stayed within our family income budgets. My mother and I would go shopping at a nearby grocery market, and she would take out food stamps to pay. Because we had little cash, I could not buy any extra items such as bubble gum, a small toy, or a candy because she did not have enough money to purchase non-essential food items. I remembered asking, "Mom, could I get this bubble gum?" But she said, "No, we do not have money for that bubble gum. We are tight for this month. Maybe next month." I said, "OK." Then, I put the bubble gum back in the aisle where the bubble gums were located. While I wanted the items, I understood that my family did not have a lot of money to spend on such things.

I wore old clothes donated to me from the Goodwill Industries International and other shirts and pants from my older brothers. I did not have allowances like other American middle-class or wealthy children. While I did not like living month by month to make it in American society, I was glad that we had enough food to eat and a place to live together as a family that was safe and clean, in comparison to our filthy and unhealthy living conditions back in the two refugee camps in Malaysia.

CHAPTER 4
MOVING TO A SUBURBAN NEIGHBORHOOD

My family and I stayed for over a year in the small apartment in Los Angeles before we moved to Monterey Park, a suburban community in the San Gabriel Valley in Southern California. That was one of the more friendly communities for my family and me, and Asian Americans generally felt welcomed there. The City of Monterey Park was considered "Little Taipei" because of the many Taiwanese residents living in that city. As former refugees, my family and I wanted to live in a community that felt closer to the Asian culture and community.

With assistance from the United States Housing and Urban Development (HUD), my family and I could stay in a condominium for an affordable rent. Because we were under the federal poverty guidelines, we received housing assistance, welfare, food stamps, and free lunch in my public school. After moving there, I was grateful to leave the small apartment in Los Angeles because I did not feel safe there. I remembered that one of my older brothers, Roger, had been physically assaulted by a local gang because he was a former refugee from

Vietnam. I was glad that my family and I moved to a different neighborhood in the City of Monterey Park.

I started my third grade, and I was eight years old then. I took a school bus to Rice Elementary School located in the nearby City of Rosemead. In third grade, I started to have more confidence in my English language skills—reading, verbal communications, and writing. As I became more confident, I started to write stories. I kept on writing so many stories that my third-grade teacher, Mrs. Y., gave me an award for the student who wrote the most stories in one semester. I was proud that I could think of so many stories to write, although I came from a refugee background and had limited English language training. My teacher said, "Good job, Cuong, on writing so many stories. You have written so many interesting stories. That is good." I said, "Thank you, Mrs. Y. I like to write, so I keep on writing stories."

I liked that my third-grade teacher was encouraging me to keep on writing, and I was glad that she was my teacher. She gave me the confidence to write stories, although I knew nothing about writing stories, especially in English.

In the Monterey Park community, I felt a sense of relief that my family and I were slowly moving up the socio-economic ladder. For example, my mother now could buy more food because my older siblings gave her some money to take care of household expenses. My older siblings were graduating from two-year and four-year colleges, and they were working to earn money. They were able to help with the family expenses such as rent, food, clothing, utilities, telephone, and water bills. My father was taking English language classes, so he could find work in the community. My mother tried to learn English, but she always liked being at home to take care of her children and the household. Although she slowly learned English, she really only wanted to find ways to support her children and her husband by being the best cook and keeping our home immaculate, all things she could do by staying in the house. This brought her great pleasure and personal satisfaction.

As for me, I really liked being in the Monterey Park community because I enjoyed going to school and getting involved in the local parks and recreation activities. I started to join a community basketball team, and I started to learn skating by playing roller hockey.

I was making new friends, including my roller hockey coach, and I enjoyed being active in sports such as basketball, flag football, track and field, as well as roller hockey. One day, my basketball coach said, "You are good at roller hockey. How come?" I replied, "I enjoy being in the outdoors, and I enjoy being active. There is nothing to do in my house, so I roller skate outside my parents' condo. So, I get to practice a lot on the roller-skating; plus, I enjoy meeting new people."

At Rice Elementary School, I began to make new friends at school as well. I was able to find a few friends that I could trust, given my shy introvert personality and the English language barrier. I played marbles with my friends and played basketball after school with them. From the third grade until I graduated from that school in the sixth grade, I continued to learn more English. I was slowly adjusting to life in the United States, yet I still felt like an "alien" or an "outsider" because I did not have blue eyes or blond hair. For example, whenever I saw cartoons or comedies on TV, I did not identify with the actors and/or actresses because I did not see many Asian faces. Nonetheless, I watched TV because I needed to learn how to speak English.

As I grew up in the Monterey Park community, I also wanted to help my parents earn extra money, so we could keep up with the rent and buy other necessities to survive in America. Hence, I worked part-time to help my family by mowing the lawn and watering the grass for the condominium association where we lived. The association paid my father money if we mowed the lawns and took care of the lawns of the different condos in the association. My father said, "After school each day on Mondays and Fridays, you have to water the lawn in the front part of the condo buildings. By watering the lawns, our family gets paid from the condo association to maintain the lawns. That is your duty." I said, "Yes, Papa. I understand. I will do it after school each Monday and Friday." I wanted to support him because as a family, we were trying to survive financially in America.

At that time, our family was still under the federal poverty line, so we continued to receive food stamps, free lunch, and welfare benefits to live. We were dependent on the benefits and health care from the federal government. Whenever I was sick from bronchitis, I used the federal government health care system to obtain medicines for bronchitis and other illnesses growing up as a teenager. My mother would take me to the doctor by using the federal government health care plan to pay for the doctor's services and for the medicines.

Along with finding ways to survive financially in America, the cultural shock of being a former refugee living in this nation caused many occasions of confusion and misunderstanding for me. One of the most memorable experiences growing up as a former refugee in the United States was the feeling of wearing two different "shirts." That is, when I was at home in my parents' home, I needed to respect my Vietnamese Chinese cultural norms and to respect what my parents and older adults would say, even at times when they were not factually correct. As the youngest of the siblings, I would dutifully listen to what my parents and other older adults would say to me. In my parents' home, I was an introvert and not very expressive of my thoughts and ideas, given my family upbringing as the youngest of my siblings.

For this main reason, my school teachers and other students considered me to be shy, introverted, not expressive, and seen as "fresh off the boat" because I was not "talkative" or expressive in the classroom and during school activities. I tended to keep my mouth shut, even though I wanted to say and express my feelings and ideas in school.

Fortunately, as I became more acculturated into American society, I began to understand the public school's norms and activities. Over time, I became more vocal in academic classes and joined after-school activities to learn how to express myself and to find my own identity.

Not surprisingly, exhausted from so many activities at school and from helping my family by doing part-time jobs to earn money, sometimes I would get confused about which cultural "shirt" I was supposed to wear. That is, I got confused with the different American cultural norms while being at home. At home, with my parents and older siblings, they thought that I was too vocal in expressing my opinions; to them, I was being "too American and talking out loud." Sometimes, I was disciplined by my older siblings and parents. For instance, they would say that, since I was the youngest, I needed to listen to the older adults and the parents because older people are wiser and know more than the younger kids. Over time, I accepted that, as a former refugee in the United States, I needed to wear two dissimilar "shirts" because I was living in two different worlds – in the American mainstream society and in my Vietnamese Chinese cultural home environment.

The situation of wearing two dissimilar "shirts" is common for hundreds of immigrant and refugee youth growing up in the United States, where the youth must juggle with many different cultural norms and expectations both inside and outside their home environments.

Despite the cultural shock of living in the United States as a former refugee, I am still very grateful to live in this country. Through all the hardships and struggles to build our lives and future in America, my parents and older siblings taught me the value of hard work, discipline, perseverance, and compassion to help others who are less fortunate.

My refugee experience in Malaysia and my early years in the United States have had a major impact on my life. They have not only taught me how certain social situations can create powerlessness and hopelessness, but they have also cultivated in me a strong desire to help people in need, especially vulnerable immigrant and refugee children in America and around the world.

CHAPTER 5
DESIRE TO BE A SERVANT LEADER

After growing up in destitution in the two refugee camps in Malaysia and in my early years resettling in the United States, I wanted to help my family and others to get out of poverty in the United States.

Because of my drive to improve my family's socio-economic poverty status, I studied hard in school and worked part-time to help my parents pay our household bills and other daily expenses to survive in our new home country. In addition to cutting our condo association lawns to earn extra cash for my parents on weekends, I also worked part-time after school for the Monterey Park Girls' and Boys' Club as a tutor for the elementary and junior high school students. Plus, I cleaned toilets and mopped the cafeteria floor at the East Los Angeles Community College located near the City of Monterey Park to earn extra cash during the summer of 1985.

Along with working part-time, fortunately, I did well in my academic classes. I graduated with honors from high school and participated in many community service activities. I started my own community service club when I was in the 10th grade at Mark Keppel High. Also, I was an HIV/AIDS speaker for the American Red Cross, and I shared important information about HIV/AIDS to my student peers in my high school and in my community of San Gabriel Valley.

Fortunately, because of my good grades, community service, and leadership activities, in 1990, I was accepted at the University of California, Los Angeles (UCLA) and received a substantial academic scholarship to attend the university. At UCLA, I majored in Sociology, with a minor in Asian American Studies. I was active in community service activities while I studied at UCLA. For example, I was active in working with immigrant communities by working as a public health volunteer for an on-campus service organization, and I served as a volunteer for the UCLA Asian Pacific Coalition.

Furthermore, at UCLA, I found my passion for doing research on poverty, especially in disadvantaged and vulnerable families such as immigrants, ethnic minorities, and urban and rural communities. I participated in the UCLA Urban Poverty and Public Policy Program in 1994 to study the effects of urban poverty in minority and immigrant communities across the nation by using the United States Census 1990 data. Moreover, I researched the HIV/AIDS issue that affected the Vietnamese community of Orange County, California. For that research, I received the UCLA President's Undergraduate Fellowship in 1994.

Because of my good academic standing at UCLA, I received the Woodrow Wilson National Summer Fellowships to study at Princeton University for the summers in 1994 and 1995. In the summer of 1995, at the Office of Population Research at Princeton University, I researched poverty among Southeast Asian Americans (e.g., Hmong, Cambodian, Laotian, and Vietnamese), using the 1990 Census data. My research findings were published in the *Asian American Policy Review*, a publication of the Harvard University Kennedy School of Government student publication in 1997.

After graduating from UCLA, I received a graduate fellowship from The University of Chicago to study public policy and finance as a Woodrow Wilson Fellow. I spent two years from 1996 to 1998 at The University of Chicago learning about public policy and the fundamentals of finance, economics, statistics, and budgeting.

Always remembering my refugee background in Malaysia, I wanted to be the best that I could be. To be a more effective servant leader, I decided to get a law degree to complement my graduate degree in public policy and finance. One of my mentors said to me once, "If you want to get your law degree, you need to do it soon. Do not listen to anyone else. If it is your dream to go to law school, aim for it. Don't wait until you are 60 years old, and then get your law degree."

But then I asked, "Are there not too many lawyers out there in America? Plus, are lawyers considered 'sharks'?"

My mentor said, "So what? Just because there are too many lawyers, does not mean that you should not get your law degree, especially if that is your dream. There are bad professionals in any industry, not only in the legal field." I told my mentor, "Yes, you are correct. I am going to plan to get my law degree."

Therefore, I enrolled at the University of California Hastings College of Law for three years, from 2000 to 2003, as a Thurgood Marshall Fellow. At Hastings College of Law, I learned the basics of how legislation and regulations are interpreted. The legal experience later helped me to found a non-profit group organized to invest in and empower refugee and immigrant youth from low-wealth backgrounds across the United States.

After graduating from law school in 2003, I was honored to be accepted into the Presidential Management Fellows (PMF) Program under the United States Office of Personnel Management (OPM). The PMF Program is a two-year leadership program for graduate students interested in leading agencies or managing programs and projects for the federal government. In August 2003, I started my work assignment with the National Aeronautics and Space Administration (NASA) with my first year under the PMF Program. In that year, I worked on budget activities for educational public outreach and space programs for NASA.

As part of my rotation assignment under the PMF Program, I went on a one-year detail assignment with the U.S. Senate Committee on Finance in August 2004. In other words, I had a great opportunity to work for one year on the U.S. Senate Committee on Finance as a Legislative Fellow under United States Senator Max Baucus from Montana. At the U.S. Senate Committee on Finance, I learned the legislative process at the federal government level.

In my final days of my detail assignment as a Legislative Fellow in the Senate Committee on Finance, U.S. Senator Max Baucus asked me, "So, what are you going to do next?"

I said, "Sir, I am going back to NASA because I gave my word to my supervisor that I would be back at the space agency after one year in the Senate Finance Committee."

Senator Baucus said, "Well, that is good; we are going to miss you."

I said, "Thank you, Senator Baucus. I love my experience in the Senate, but I have to go back to NASA because of my promise to my supervisor that I shall be going back to the space agency. It has been an honor to see what has been going on in the U.S. Senate for this past year." In looking back, I learned so much about the federal legislative process as a Legislative Fellow with the U.S. Senate Committee on Finance.

At the conclusion of my detail assignment, I returned to NASA. For a period of nine years after leaving the Senate Committee on Finance, I worked on budget, project management, education and public outreach, and policy issues and activities for the senior officials at NASA. I also had a chance to see the Space Shuttle launch at the Kennedy Space Center in Florida of the Hubble Space Telescope as a NASA civil servant employee. My NASA professional working activities were some of the most pleasant and memorable experiences of my career as a professional in the federal government.

However, my NASA career did not allow me to focus on and invest in the refugee and immigrant youth, specifically those coming from low-wealth backgrounds and households. Given my personal experience as a former refugee, I felt drawn to investing and supporting the refugee and immigrant youth and their families. In 2011, I decided to found a non-profit organization to invest in and support the vulnerable youth, especially those coming from low-wealth backgrounds. The name of this non-profit is called the Enlightened Initiative (EI).

The three major goals of EI are: (1) building leadership skills for the refugee and immigrant youth; (2) empowering the youth to learn Science, Technology, Engineering, Arts, Math, and Mental Wellness (STEAM2) disciplines so they can be innovators; and (3) fostering positive inter-racial relationships to prepare these vulnerable youth to lead in a complex American society. I wanted to create the Enlightened Initiative because I want to invest in and support the youth to have the confidence to go after their dreams and to be leaders in their communities and families in the United States.

Since 2011, Enlightened Initiative (EI) has substantially impacted many vulnerable youth. EI has helped many young immigrants and refugees from low-wealth households to reach their full potential by helping them to (1) obtain scholarships to attend universities; (2) support them to lead school clubs and activities, and (3) encourage them to be involved in their communities such as serving others who are less fortunate. Many of the youth who have attended EI have taken leadership positions in school clubs that serve the community have received academic financial scholarships in their undergraduate and graduate schools. EI is making a substantial positive difference in the lives of these immigrant and refugee youths throughout the nation.

Because of my current involvement with the Enlightened Initiative, I am constantly looking for ways to invest in and support these vulnerable young immigrants and refugees. Due to my involvement with and investments into the youth, I received the prestigious W.K. Kellogg Foundation Fellowship from 2014-2016. This Fellowship allowed me to increase my effectiveness as a non-profit founder to grow the Enlightened Initiative and to invest in the youth across the nation and Puerto Rico.

The next step in investing and empowering the youth was to write a book about them. As I talked to one of my mentors and with the youth themselves, they would encourage me to write a book. In one of the EI summer leadership camp sessions held in Washington, D.C., the youth would say that they wanted me to write the book because the American public needs to know the stories of the young immigrants and refugees like them. I told the youth, "I agree."

My story of coming to America and my early years of resettlement in the United States is similar to the other youth who came here from various countries around the world such as Mexico, Ecuador, El Salvador, Vietnam, China, Haiti, Dominican Republic, and Argentina. The youth's stories demonstrate their courage, resilience, commitment, hardships, obstacles, hard work, perseverance, patience, determination, and love for their families, friends, and communities.

The following chapters of this book are the stories of the young immigrants and refugees who have gone through Enlightened Initiative (a non-profit organization), their backgrounds, their experiences, and their lives. Each chapter illustrates the story of a single young immigrant or refugee who has gone through God's crucible to become who they are: hard-working youth who want the best education, health care, housing, and opportunities for themselves and for their families in their new homeland called the United States of America. Only their first names are disclosed here; their last names have been kept confidential to respect their privacy as they shared their stories.

PART II
IMMIGRANT AND REFUGEE YOUTH'S STORIES

CHAPTER 6
"MAX"
DISASTER, DETERMINATION,
AND DESTINY

They found me hiding in the bathroom trying to finish my homework. They walked me at gunpoint into the room where my mom stood trembling in fright. The gunman and robbers stole family heirlooms, passports, and visas, and traumatized the entire family. These vandals took much more from us than our material belongings. They took our right to live in our native country of Haiti and to decrease our future aspirations. My mother sacrificed her career as a physician in Haiti and immigrated to the United States to start anew in hopes of a safer and more secure future for us all.

Our family's education and profession as medical doctors gave the false impression of wealth. This outward perception probably targeted our home for the robbery. Frightened by the events of that fateful night resulted in a more tragic demise than some lost material belongings. Our family felt forced to flee. We sought refuge in a place that promised more security and stability in the United States. While no place is without its flaws, some countries are more promising than others. The United States was a beacon of such promise, apprehensively chosen by my mother. This led to a fatherless home, given my father's unwillingness to sacrifice his professional career in Haiti.

Soon after this event in August 2004, my twin brother and I flew with my mother to Florida for a short summer vacation and made the life-altering decision to remain in the United States permanently. My twin brother and I matriculated into the second grade a few weeks later with no knowledge of the English language. Not only did we have to adjust to a new country, but we also had to do so without speaking the English language. Fortunately, we were resourceful, resilient, and tenacious. We learned to adjust to the American social norms, cultural differences, and nuanced social structure of Boca Raton, Florida.

Within a year, I was up-to-par with my native counterparts in the English language, and by the 5th grade, I moved into more fast-paced courses. My teacher at the time, Ms. Taylor, inspired my interest in the sciences with her assertion that the boundless universe is within our grasp if our quest is guided by the tools offered by science. Her inspiration and faith in my abilities led me to apply and subsequently be accepted into to Boca Raton Middle School's Pre-Med Academy.

How fortunate to have this the unparalleled opportunity in such a specialized program. The rigidity of the curriculum not only taught me discipline in my academic pursuits, but also allowed me to further advance in science, technology, engineering, and math (STEM) fields with advanced science and mathematics course work. My success in the program led me to apply and be accepted to one of Florida's most affluent secondary institutions: Suncoast Community High School, a school that is currently ranked #61 nationally, #6 in Florida, and #14 in magnet high schools by *U.S News and World Report* by then.

Suncoast administrators at that high school first assigned me to its most rigorous program, the Math Science and Engineering (MSE) program. I did not find the coursework to interest me and decided to transfer to the International Baccalaureate (IB) program.

There was also uncertainty in how we were going to fund my post-secondary education. I graduated from my high school with honors in 2014. I was awarded the Gates Millennium Scholarship and being named a Quest Bridge Finalist.

As a result, I matriculated to Emory University as a dual academic scholar: a Gates Millennium Scholar and a Quest Bridge Scholar. That college experience was not a smooth one, but trials and tribulations have only ensured that I remain focused on my eventual goal of following in my parents' footsteps to become a physician. I majored in Neuroscience and Behavioral Biology, with a minor in Music, and graduated from Emory with a Bachelor's in Science in May of 2018. I continued on to their Master's in Public Health Program at the Rollins School of Public Health and am currently a first-year graduate student in their Behavioral Science and Health Education Program on track to graduate in the Spring of 2020. Through the grace of God and hard work, I was blessed with the opportunity to attend college loan-free. The support system provided by my family also made the hardships we faced bearable.

As I now sit and reflect upon my experience as a child, I can say that my circumstances have improved personally, but conditions have deteriorated rapidly for Haiti. I am now an aspiring physician currently learning the skillset of a public health practitioner. I hope to heal others through medicine, as my mother once did before that fateful night's robbery back in Haiti.

My professional pursuits have given me the opportunity to affect my surroundings: to better the immigrant youth who come after me. As for my native country in Haiti, political turmoil has eaten away at the democracy that once existed. The infamous earthquake in 2010 placed the country in more peril than had existed earlier, and those who prey on the innocent, just as they did with me so long ago, only weaken the country further.

In some ways, the situation in Haiti did improve; in some ways it did not. What is certain is that my career prospects arose from my mother's sacrifices. The conditions back in Haiti have inspired me to fight oppression in a time to come. The tools I have gained through education and working through tough obstacles have equipped me to join those leading changes to better our world. It is an opportunity made possible due to an incredible support system and mentors that continue to inspire me to succeed.

Lastly, in reflecting on the positives of growing up as an immigrant youth in America, I can say unequivocally that the United States is a country of opportunity. Despite its flaws rooted in a history of racism and oppression, it is still a land of possibility. We, as immigrants today, can only fight to improve the chance for success of those who come after us. I will always be grateful for the privilege I have had to pursue an education and the resources available to facilitate my success as a future physician.

CHAPTER 7
"THO"
BÀ NGOẠI'S (GRANDMA'S) EXAMPLE

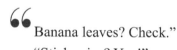Banana leaves? Check."

"Sticky rice? Yup!"

"Fatty pork? Got it!"

Ready to make *banh tet*, a traditional dish for Vietnamese New Year, alongside my grandmother, Bà *ngoại*, I watched her carefully. With her adept hands, Bà *ngoại* sprinkled the rice onto the glistening banana leaves, creating a thick layer of milky grains. She then layered the mung beans on the rice. She meticulously positioned a sturdy strip of fatty pork on the top. With a flip of her hands, *Bà* fluidly rolled and wrapped all the ingredients inside the banana leaves.

Watching *Bà ngoại*'s hands crafting the log-like roll, I attempted to follow her steps to make a *banh tet* (Vietnamese sweetened cake), but grains of rice scattered everywhere. *Bà* gave me that scolding look. At once, my mind said, "Clean up and get out of here!" but a weathered look on *Bà ngoại's* face caught my eyes. *Bà* was tired, too. *Bà* stayed. I was tired, so I, too, stayed to complete the task at hand.

Unlike me, my grandma was raised by our ancestors' rule, as sacred as the traditional recipe of *banh tet*. Her childhood unfolded in the kitchen, the outdoor market, and the sewing room, while mine was studying at school, roaming the paddy fields, and playing with the neighborhood children.

I was born and raised in Vietnam. I immigrated with my parents to Northern Virginia when I was 12 years old. I am an only child. My parents often joked that I was hard to rear as a child, so they stopped having kids after me. I was restless and determined, curious and tenacious.

As an adolescent, I didn't battle with daily hunger. I had come to the world's wealthiest country, the United States of America. Despite the gap in our ages, *Bà ngoại* and I shared one identity: exile. As an immigrant in America, I felt like an outcast in this new world. Pushed to a distant village when the Vietnam War broke out, *Bà*, on the other hand, struggled to rebuild her life while still in her home country, and through that adversity, she developed perseverance, diligence, and resilience, all of which radiate today, especially when she makes *banh tet*. From *Bà ngoại*, I learned that hardship teaches an important lesson: Life presents challenges, and I must overcome and recover from them. I apply this maxim to my life by challenging myself, working diligently, while remaining flexible in both my personal life and academic studies. Uprooted from the familiarity of my homeland to immigrate to America was the most significant challenge that life has given me. Stripped of my language and culture, I shivered, feeling existentially naked, facing discrimination and isolation as an immigrant in America. Confused and lonely, I didn't know how to react in my new country.

The first couple of years in America were tough. The language barrier and discrimination against Southeast Asians made it difficult for my parents to find jobs. We all struggled, but during that first a year, I quickly acquired enough English to navigate in our new country. My parents could never quite overcome the English language barrier. To this day, comfort communicating in English still hinders my parents from fully participating in American society.

Nevertheless, reflecting on Grandma's strength, I diligently launched myself into academic studies. Steadily expanding my vocabulary and comprehension of English, I studied, participated, and enthusiastically asked questions at school. My thick accent didn't stop me from conversing with classmates to make friends and to hone my English pronunciation words. *Bà ngoại's* example worked for me; despite initial adversity, I quickly assimilated into my new surroundings in America. Through the challenges of being an immigrant presented, I discovered within me a seed-like interest in mathematics. Thanks to this universal language, I could communicate ideas and logic despite the language barrier and this seed took root. This appreciation for mathematics soon budded into a keen fervor. I blossomed with pleasure, solving math problems and proofing theorems.

Mind-boggled with Euclid's proof and Euler's formula, I learned experimental math, which later flowered into my interest in engineering. Because of this passion, I often found myself attracted to numerous sciences, technology, engineering, and math (STEM) programs during my four years in high school. Despite my enthusiasm, at times, these STEM programs added stress to my busy life and drove me to the brink of giving up. Nevertheless, reflecting on *Bà ngoại*, persevering in the face of adversity, I embraced the challenges. Failure was not an option. I refused to stop trying.

Preparing for the Vietnamese New Year celebration that time years ago, despite *Bà ngoại's* initial disappointment, I began the process of making *banh tet* again. I meticulously layered the rice, mung beans, and fatty pork on the banana leaves. I rolled everything into a log before wrapping it with a string. At last, following *Bà's* instruction and work ethic, our preparation was complete. It was going to be a good New Year.

Despite the initial hardship, our Vietnamese American family is happy here. We now have a house, food on our table, and jobs that earn enough money to sustain our quality of life. Together, we celebrate our accomplishments, such as my admittance to the Massachusetts Institute of Technology (MIT) after graduating from high school. It was I who was accepted into MIT, but it was definitely teamwork with my parents. Despite not knowing how school works in America, they, along with my teachers and mentors, support me with generosity and love.

One of the mottos I heard somewhere is to: "Find yourself mentors wherever you are and for whatever you do." As cliché as it sounds, I am learning to surround myself with people who make me a more curious, motivated, hard-working, or better version of myself.

I may be older, but I still have some naive and emotional part in me. This view of the world gave me hope to do unexpected things: mastering English quickly, succeeding in high school, getting into MIT, getting an Electrical Engineering/Computer Science degree at MIT, and then getting accepted into MIT's Master of Engineering program.

In looking backing at my personal experiences, I do not think I would be that hungry for knowledge, education, and self-transformation if I had not been thrown into American society as an immigrant youth from Vietnam. There was something about my age at that time that played a critical role in this story. I was young, naive, and emotional. I still believed in fairytales. I believed that I could rise above the challenges as an underdog, taking everyone by surprise. Everyone, of course, except my grandmother. *Bà ngoại* taught me persistence pays off.

CHAPTER 8
"JONATHAN S."
FINALLY!

The day of our flight finally arrived. We were full of expectations. I was 15 years old, leaving Ecuador and going to the United States to live with my dad and older sister. How long I had waited for this day. How much I longed to have a father-son relationship with my dad again. We honestly knew that it might be difficult at first because of how long we had lived apart, but at the same time, we were excited because deep inside of us we desired to be together again.

When we finally got to John F. Kennedy International Airport in New York, my dad and sister came to welcome us. We had not seen each other for many years, so it was a beautiful moment when we saw them again. When we arrived at our house, one of my aunts from my mom's side was waiting for us with a big, delicious breakfast that we gobbled up completely. Everything was so good to eat! It seemed that my dream since I was a kid — to have a solid, true family — was fulfilled.

Little did I know that was just the beginning of what was coming. As time passed, problems and conflicts within my family began to develop. The five of us lived in a stuffy, cramped attic. Little by little, arguments started to arise. Having lived apart so long, my parents had grown apart and could not communicate very well with each other. My mother and father had very different opinions about what and how things should be done. Whatever one said or did, the other would disagree.

My sister, who had been in the United States for some time, lived with us, too, but she was seldom at home. We did not have much opportunity to become close to each other. Even my brother, who had come with my mom and me from Ecuador, and I stopped sharing our secrets and conversations with each other as we had before we arrived in the United States. Each of us in the family shut ourselves off from the others to escape the turmoil arising in our home because of the miscommunications and unfulfilled expectations of all five of us living together. Months went by and things just got worse and worse because we were not communicating and understanding each other.

One night when I least expected it, my life changed radically. I went to the church where my aunt who was a pastor. My mom, brother, and I had always gone to church before coming to the United States. My mother had grown up practicing Christianity. I, too, had gone to church since I was young but never really paid much attention to who God is, what He wanted from me, and what He could do with and for me. Religion was not something I cared much about; it was more a tradition than anything else. However, that night something changed. After coming home from a youth service, I felt something I had never felt before — a desire to seek God arose within me. I went into my sister's room and prayed non-stop.

Something happened. I became a totally different person. Since then, I have begun to develop an intimate relationship with God. I enjoy spending time with Him, just talking to Him, getting to know Him more and more. It became a passion. In that relationship, He did things in me that I never thought anybody would do for me. He removed from my heart the resentment that I had towards my family.

God taught me to love myself and to love my family, even when I felt I had reason to hate them. And through that love, God healed my heart. I now can truthfully say to my family, "I love you."

As I spent more time with God and sought His guidance in my life, I noticed my family also started to change. We have all cried together, asking for forgiveness and giving big hugs to each other. We realized that God loved us first, and we could learn to love one another as a family.

It has been almost three years since God became my reason for being. I now realize that God was always present in my family; I see it clearly now. Finally, I can thank God, my family, my aunt, and other amazing people from my church who have helped and encouraged me to keep believing there was more for me and my family! I feel more confident facing the challenges of immigrating from Ecuador, coming to the United States as a teenager, and living as a family who had been separated for such a long time.

With God's help, I am overcoming my timidity, which is typical of immigrant youth. I had been reluctant even to exert the effort to fit into the American mainstream society. It hurt to be misunderstood because I was an "outsider." Earlier, I didn't want to push myself to learn or try new things. It was embarrassing to speak English when I knew I would say things that would not make sense. It was lonely outside my comfort zone. I shied away from new challenges at first but soon realized that hurts would later heal over time. I had to make the move to thrive in this American culture and not only to survive in it. Taking such leaps might hurt to get out of my comfort zone, but stepping out to show my true personality and my identity have been worth it.

Despite the obstacles of living in the United States and the negative feelings I have had, I now see things in a more positive light. I used to withdraw and stay in the shadows. In my country, Ecuador, I just thought of myself as any other youth in the crowd — I was no one special, living a normal life, having the opportunity to go school, but that was it. However, having left Ecuador, growing up as an immigrant youth in the United States, I am learning to face and overcome challenges, and to see that I have more to give and that I am not just a face in the crowd. I am no longer satisfied giving up when tired, frustrated, embarrassed, or even being hurt by others. Because of these experiences, I see that I can make a difference. This is not because I am any more special than other immigrant youth, but because I am discovering who I truly am and have the potential to be: a servant leader under the leadership of Mighty God.

For these reasons, I want to encourage all immigrant youth reading this book to not give up on their dreams. If you had to move from your country of origin to a new country, it was for a purpose. Even if right now things are not going the way you wish they would, it does not mean that they are going to be like this forever. You are valuable and important, gifted and special. Just believe in yourself, and, with God's help, you will do what you dream to do!

CHAPTER 9
"NEFTALI"
ADIOS Y HOLA

Life in the United States started for me on March 29, 2001, the day my family reached California. I was born in Manzanillo, Colima in the country of Mexico, where I spent the first seven years of my life with my mom and sister, Yesica. Dad had gone to the United States to find work and, for two years, was sending money for us to live in Mexico. Then he came back to Mexico.

After one year of living back in Manzanillo, Dad decided to move the whole family up to the United States. So, *Adios, Mexico*! *Hola América!*

I mainly missed my grandma. She had been my primary caretaker. I loved her cooking. I just wanted to go back home. Food in California was so different. I didn't like it at all. But within two weeks, after getting the requisite vaccinations, my parents enrolled me in school in America. What a shock! It was months before I could even understand what was going on: The English language, the American culture, and the loneliness!

The next school year, in the English as a second language class (ESL), I dedicated myself to learning the language. That hard work paid off and when I no longer needed a teaching assistant translating for me, the principal assigned me to regular academic classes.

Growing up in a neighborhood with mainly Latino families proved to be a bonus for a Mexican family like ours. When Rose Espinoza, a non-profit founder, first opened her garage to kids in her neighborhood, offering them a place to go to avoid gangs and to consider college, she didn't think it would last. I'm glad it did. Rose's program was there to help us with regular homework and academic projects. Rosie's Garage, a non-profit founded by Rose Espinoza, was open on Saturdays and Sundays. That was great. I hate to procrastinate. At Rosie's Garage, I could do all my school projects and homework before the due dates. This kept me from stressing out. *"Hola, el garaje de Rosie."*

Though most of our Latino parents wanted to help, few of them understood enough English to be of much assistance. Thanks to Rosa and her organization, I was able to earn and maintained a 3.7 GPA throughout middle school and high school when I graduated in 2012.

Now, that I am just two semesters away from receiving my bachelor's degree in entertainment and tourism, I look back and am truly proud of myself, given that I have overcome many obstacles as a young immigrant. But for me, to prove myself to others, I need to accomplish a lot in the future. First, I must finish the university while working two jobs and without incurring any student debt. *"Hola libertad financiera."*

With all these great things happening and the bright future ahead, there still are dark days. As an undocumented immigrant youth, I cannot leave the country to visit family members. In 2016, just when I was going to graduate with my Associate of Arts degree from community college, my family received a call from Mexico. My grandma had passed away. They wanted us to come for the services. We could not go. We were afraid; we might not have been able to return to the United States.

How sad we were. It was hard for me not being able to say good-bye to my grandma. She was like my mother to me, caring for me during those first seven years of life until my family and I came to America; there was no "*Adios, abuela*" to my grandmother. It was hard seeing my Dad crying because we could not go to Mexico because of our undocumented legal status. He never had a chance to say, "*Adios, mama.*"

Despite my education, because of my undocumented legal status, I worried. What if ended up working at a warehouse or in landscaping or a fast food place, just like many undocumented people, including my family members? I constantly feel the pressure to prove to other people that we belong here in the United States of America. We are not here in America to take away native-born American people's jobs. I sometimes question myself if what I am doing at the end will be worth it or should if I should just quit now and go back to Mexico.

It's difficult to stay focused when I hear people calling us "rapists" or/and "criminals," when, in reality, we are not. We are just regular human beings trying to provide for ourselves by working hard and be good human beings in the American society. True, some people from the Latino community do get in trouble with the law, but generalizing that all Latinos like me are "bad people" is wrong and can be hurtful. My family and I are here in America just trying to live our lives. We, as their children, want to provide for ourselves, so we can start our own families and be able to take care of our parents.

Because of the many obstacles growing up as an undocumented youth in America, observers sometimes wonder if there is anything positive left for undocumented youth. I say yes. In my neighborhood, there is Rosie's Garage. Along the way, people have come along with us to cheer us on. They inspire us to not give up so easily just because we may not have a "green card." They tell us not to worry when we feel like, "What's the point? I can't go to college. It's too expensive and I cannot afford it." Instead, they direct us to non-profits that want to help undocumented teenagers like me. What I have learned in school and in my community is mine to use for a lifetime.

Just when I thought I was done with school, President Barack Obama ordered an executive action to create the Deferred Action for Childhood Arrivals (DACA) program that really helped me a lot. As a DACA participant, I could apply for scholarships where a Social Security number was not required. I had been involved in my high school activities, so I was able to get good recommendation letters from my teachers. Before I finished my senior year in high school, I was awarded three scholarships. This financial assistance helped me a lot during my first year of community college. However, the DACA status is still tenuous. There is no pathway to full American citizenship yet. DACA documents have to be renewed every two or three years. The DACA applications are expensive, too.

I know that my family members are proud of what we have been able to do as a family. My undocumented hard-working parents who did not finish high school now has a son who will get a Certificate in Radio Broadcasting and an Associate of Arts Degree in Radio Broadcasting. I am just a few months away from reaching a huge milestone for all of my family members by receiving my bachelor's degree in Entertainment and Tourism in May of 2019. The journey has not been easy, but it has been a fun ride. I am learning a lot from my professors and my friends so far along this journey.

What else can I say about my 18 years in the United States? The journey has not been easy, but the trying times have helped me to become a strong, well-developed young man. Reflecting on the successes over the year, I realize I am worth the effort, more self-confident, and revel in the power of education. I am truly living my own American dream. It's all thanks to my parents for always being there and for always supporting me. At the end of the day, it will be "Our American dream." So, *Hola América.* I am here to stay!

CHAPTER 10
"ELIZABETH"
HOPE AFTER HURRICANE MARIA

Hurricane Irma had already come and gone, and now we heard news that Hurricane Maria was on the way! These were not long lost cousins who visited us, but hurricanes that devastated my home country of Puerto Rico! In August 2017, the news started to inform us that a tropical storm would soon become a hurricane named Irma. Irma became a Category 3 hurricane with winds of 185 kilometer per hour, and Irma poured heavy torrents of rain on my community. Because of the hurricane, my mother, brother, and I had to take refuge in a school. We had already spent a week without electricity, and when the electricity came back, the news media blasted that there was another Hurricane Maria brewing on a storm path to our island.

Hurricane Maria destroyed the infrastructure of the island. Currently, Puerto Rico is still recovering from this disaster. Torrential rain and winds damaged houses, schools, forests, animals, and killed hundreds of people in Puerto Rico. I remembered emerging from the shelter in the middle of the night and looking around in horror. There were no lights to see details of the destruction, but I could see that all the trees near me were broken. As the sun rose, it was clear that three of my neighbors lost their homes. Also, two broken doors to my home let in water causing a soggy mess everywhere inside my home.

It was the unforgettable sensory images of Hurricane Maria that brought tears to my eyes. The whistle of the winds through the trees and the whipping off rooftops were constant. The persistent pounding of the rain was unrelenting. The high-pitched crying of little children never stopped. My family and I had tastelessness of the government-issued food. The physical exhaustion and the heat were unbearable, and we waited for up to six hours just to get fresh water. Then, the sound of weary weeping that comes with loss of human lives and the depletion of money and resources linger still. The experiences were unforgettable and heartbreaking to me and to thousands of other Puerto Ricans.

Because of Hurricane Maria, my mother decided to send me to the United States with my aunt who lives in New Jersey, so I would not have to lose track in my academic studies. Of course, at first, I refused to leave my mother, but the decision for me to go to the United States was not mine to make. My mother had already decided what was best for me.

When I first arrived in the United States, I started with the school process, and the school was so big that I got scared. However, the school secretary was very understanding and nice to me. She talked to me in Spanish to make me feel comfortable in the new school setting.

My mother stayed with me that first day of school, but the next day she returned to Puerto Rico. In my school, there were a lot more students who were immigrants than white Americans. Fortunately, a nice teacher helped me to adjust in finding the right classes. By looking at other immigrant students in my school, I realized that I was not alone. We, the immigrant students, were in the school for a reason – to build a strong future for ourselves and for our families.

In addition to adjusting to life in New Jersey, the English language and the American culture, there were the seasons. I had to learn to speak English well. Plus, I did not know many other students in my school; hence, I felt sad. At times, I felt overwhelmed, and I cried. I didn't know how to dress for school because there are four seasons in New Jersey. In Puerto Rico, I only had to consider clothes for the warm temperatures, given the island has more stable warm temperatures. I wanted to go back home to Puerto Rico!

The duties to overcome obstacles and hardships, become independent at an early age, and try to succeed without disappointing my family members and friends caused significant stress for me. However, knowing what happened to Puerto Rico because of Hurricane Maria, I knew that I had to make tough decisions to live in the United States.

The weight felt heavier because I felt all alone. To keep my "proper" attitude and to keep me motivated to stay focused on the good of this bad thing of not seeing my mother, I always say this to myself, "This is best for me and for my family; nobody has opportunities like these that I have." I repeat to myself, "It is not easy, but we must go forward. We cannot change the past, but we can change and decide on our future."

Despite feeling the pressures to succeed as an immigrant youth in the United States, I do love the education that I am receiving in New Jersey. I want to learn to be an animator and maybe a writer. Despite the storms that devastated my hometown on the island of Puerto Rico and going to school here in the United States, I am learning to communicate better in English and becoming less self-conscious about speaking with a Spanish accent. Most of all, I have hope for the future. One day, I may be able to return to Puerto Rico in order to aid in the recovery to help the people of Puerto Rico after the major hurricane.

CHAPTER 11
"GISSELLE"
CIRCLES OF DIFFERENT SIZES

Born into a large family in Argentina, encircled by love and joy, what a shock to my four year old self when hate and horror forced us to flee. My mother's store was robbed multiple times. The financial recession in Argentina jeopardized my father's job. My parents decided something had to change, so they decided to tear our nuclear family away, hopped on a plane, immigrated to New York, and joined my grandfather and uncle who already had established themselves there.

Everything in New York City excited me – the lights, the tall buildings, and the number of people in the crowded streets. Within a few months of arriving into America, I started school. Then, suddenly, I felt a new shock. Everything was unfamiliar to me, and my mother was leaving me there. I knew no one at school. I could not speak the English language. I wandered around lost and alone all day in my school.

My home life in America changed, too. Even with the addition of a new baby brother, we did not find much comfort in that somewhat enlarged circle. Home in America became a lonely place. My father worked long hours. My mother scrambled to learn English herself. My two-year-old sister and I were used to being in a large family back in Argentina. It was just so hard to adjust to life without lots of aunts, uncles, and cousins bounding around and encircling us. I often wondered if we even belonged here in America with so few family members around us and even fewer close friends.

When I was ten years old, my mother revealed that we did not have legal documents to remain in the United States. Oh my! That meant no one in our family could travel freely, openly seek for a better job, or even get a license to drive.

Shame shadowed my days and fear cloaked my nights. I remembered not wanting to mention to classmates at school anything about our illegal immigration status. I was afraid of what they might say to the authorities. It is hard to fall asleep when swirling thoughts about being deported darkened each day. This is because my baby brother was born here. He is an American citizen. If the rest of us (e.g., my two parents and my sister and I) were forced to return to Argentina, my baby brother would be left in the United States in an even smaller family circle.

Fear and shame continued to haunt me during my teenage years. I could not talk to anyone about my immigration situation. All of my friends are native-born Americans -- how could they understand what I was going through? Instead, I tried to keep in touch with those we left back home in Argentina. We made phone calls and had Skype visits with extended family members in Argentina. But seeing them on the computer often made me sadder. How I longed to be celebrating the holidays and birthdays with my cousins, aunts, and uncles. They felt our absence, too. We would often end Skype sessions or phone calls with, "One day we will be able to see each other again." Oh, I do hope so!

My parents always told my siblings and me that the reason that we had to leave our family in Argentina was to come to the United States

– *"para darles un futuro mejor"* ("to give you a better future"). It was difficult to imagine a better future when we lived in such a small circle – the solitary Latino family in the small New York town. Yet, I could see my parents struggling to make ends meet day in and day out. Fortunately, there was no shortage of love in my family. That certainly added a little sunshine, making a significant difference for me.

Still, as a child born outside the United States, I would be hurt by comments about immigrants and illegal aliens. For a long time, I wished that my family had never chosen to leave our family circle in Argentina to come to the United States. The nasty comments from others and graphic images in television sets hit hard because the truth is that my family was here illegally. But could that be so bad when my parents' motives were so good? My parents did not believe they had a choice if we had not immigrated to the United States. Personally, I thought it would have been easier to stay with family back home in Argentina.

I didn't like being labeled the "illegal immigrant" described in my history textbook. How could I stand tall when classmates and neighbors who would see me as the "bad person" that television news shows would illustrate teenagers like me as "illegal immigrants," just because I had not been born in the United States? Hearing those labels and stereotypes of immigrants and the words "illegal aliens" cast dampening clouds over who I am as a person. Who wants to be forced to identify oneself as an "illegal alien"? Not me.

Finally, in 2015, I was able to get my Deferred Action for Childhood Arrivals (DACA) paperwork. I now am "legal." I have my life here in the United States, but I still dream of the day that I will be finally able to return to Argentina and rejoin the larger family circle there. For now, I will turn my attention to the present. I can get a work permit and get a job. I can go to college. I can come out of the shadows, and I can work to fulfill my own dreams and those of my parents — that is, until it's time to renew my DACA papers. I hope the law stays in place. I hope we have the money to renew the DACA applications. And, I do hope the government passes a law so I can become a citizen of the United States. I want to contribute to the American society.

Growing up as an immigrant youth in New York has not been a "walk in the park," but I know the difficulties and struggles I experienced will one day pay off, due to my hard work, consistency, resilience, and diligence. Despite, or because of, the obvious struggles I have faced, I have learned to adapt. Coming to the United States, knowing only the Spanish language, was a challenge for me.

However, once I started school, I learned quickly how to read, write, and speak in English, even how to say the "s" sound that is so different from the sibilant "s" in the Spanish we Argentinians speak. I soon learned the subtleties of English and the odd pronunciations that look nothing like the letters that spell the words in that language.

Over time, I am learning what to do and how to navigate within the culture of this country. Consequently, I encountered few problems transitioning from middle school to high school to community college.

Since those early years, my world has expanded. You see, I now realize it is fine being an Argentinian American. I am becoming more comfortable in the newly expanded circles that include classmates and teachers, neighbors and coworkers, as well as special friends.

I look forward to fully integrating into American society. I hope to work as a professional in marine biology. I want to add my talents to assist with marine life and be a contributing member of American society. In America, I am able to go after my dream of working in marine life.

CHAPTER 12
"ANTHONY"
EITHER, OR, OR BOTH

As a first-generation American citizen, I sometimes experience an identity crisis. I am American, but my parents were not born in America. At the same time, I am a Dominican Republic person through my parents but am different because I was brought up in American culture. I think many first generation citizens share this same struggle, growing in between the two cultures and their ethnic traditions.

To share with you my background as an immigrant youth from the Dominican Republic, I first want to share my connection with the non-profit, the Enlightened Initiative (EI).

My experience with the EI program opened my mind to a whole new way of thinking and approaching life. I learned how to challenge myself through a combination of critical thinking, communication, and leadership. The sessions at EI were filled with insightful discussions that generated questions on how to reach my optimal potential. Inspiring speakers and staff members shared their own inspirational stories. The staff members of EI are some of the humblest and most generous people I have ever come across. Their passion for helping students like me in need of guidance provided a light on my journey through my life.

The EI program influenced many aspects of life that I didn't learn at home or at school. I'm still connected with the EI staff members, which demonstrates the love they have for their students and their mission. In EI, I was taught the importance of setting goals and learning self-awareness that motivated me to develop and assume leadership roles, thus preparing me for future positions to make a positive impact in the American society.

What the EI program offered was plenty of opportunity to connect with students from all over the country that have unique stories and backgrounds. I was invited to the program as a student staff member for the summer in 2012. I shared my experiences with the group of students attending the camp and helped them learn how to apply the new leadership skills gained to their lives. Little did I know that these skills were preparing me for one of the most serious and devastating events in my life.

On my last night of the camp, I received a phone call from my mother, informing that my father had been in a life-threatening accident and he might not survive. A car hit my father on his walk home from work. As a result, my father suffered a fractured skull, which affected his reasoning, ability to speak, behavior, and memory. He was in intensive care for one month and remained in the hospital for a few more months.

My father was unable to work, so our family's income plummeted. My mother, brother, and I had to step up to pay the bills, which became challenging as I was also close to embarking on my college career. Thankfully, my father recovered significantly from the accident after two years and a myriad of therapies. However, his current income is a fraction of what it used to be.

During my senior year of high school, while many students were focused on applying to universities, I was focused on working to help my family. I ruled out applying to universities. Instead, I decided to go to a community college for my first two years of college and transfer to a university after receiving my Associate of Arts (AA) degree. I chose this route because class credits were half the price at a community college compared to a university and would still count towards my bachelor's degree.

I decided to go to Palm Beach State College (PBSC) in Boca Raton, Florida, because it was close to home and seemed like the best college to attend in my area. During my first two years of college, I experienced a lot of issues with the financial aid offices at PBSC. At this time, my family income fell under $20,000 but I was still denied grants from financial aid, so I had to keep working to pay for my classes.

I was constantly stressed from managing the struggles of making enough money to support myself, helping my family, and still having a social life. I began prioritizing work and social life, becoming less engaged with the classes that I was taking. As a result, my academic grades started slipping.

At this point in my college career, I didn't know what I wanted to study. As time went by, I took the entire core classes required for my AA degree. Towards my second year, I reached a roadblock in my college career. I got to the point where my remaining classes were prerequisite elective classes. These classes went toward the bachelors' degree I was majoring in. My only problem was that I wasn't sure what I wanted to major in. I was nervous about taking classes for a major that I might not end up pursuing. Doing so would be a waste of time and money.

As the fall semester approached, I got the news that I was denied financial aid again. At this point, I began working more hours and saw an opportunity to take time off from school to focus on making money while figuring out what I wanted to major in. I always had in my mind that I would finish college, and it was always a priority. As much as I explained this to my parents, they always pressured me to continue to study and not take time off from school. Since they did not finish college, they were worried I would follow the same path as what they did.

On my year off from college, I began to get work in modeling and started building a network in the fashion industry. I got connected with people in marketing and advertising through different modeling jobs and mutual connections in the industry. I was very fascinated with the business aspect of the modeling jobs. I did my research and discovered my desire to major in business marketing. I enrolled in classes for the following fall semester that were prerequisites to the college of business. When I returned to school, I was focused and determined to excel in my classes.

In my last year at PBSC, I got straight A's for both semesters. I was set on going to Florida Atlantic University (FAU) for my Bachelor of Business Administration Degree in Marketing. Before attending FAU, I researched the top college marketing organizations. I wanted to join an organization to learn and practice hands-on marketing skills, build a professional network, and gain leadership experience.

I was most drawn by the American Marketing Association (AMA), so I decided to reach out to the chapter to make sure I could join in the upcoming fall semester. I emailed the advisor that was listed for AMA. I found out that the FAU chapter of AMA had been closed since 2013. I was determined to be a part of this reputable marketing organization, so I worked with the advisor for the organization to re-establish the chapter.

After three months of processing paperwork, strategizing, and recruiting students, I found out that another student was also working on re-establishing the AMA chapter. We worked together to restart the American Marketing Association chapter at FAU. I became a co-founder and Vice President of the American Marketing Association. I organized meetings, recruited students, processed paperwork, set up events, spoke to potential sponsors, spoke publicly, and held presentations to build up the AMA organization.

I was able to apply many of the foundational values and skills I learned in the Enlightened Initiative summer leadership camp directly to my leadership role with AMA. Additionally, from Spring 2017 to early Fall 2017, I started a marketing internship at a digital marketing firm called Rand Marketing. In my senior year at FAU, I became the President of the American Marketing Association.

Furthermore, I got a job with Amazon as a brand ambassador for their Prime Student brand. My partner and I were responsible for setting up events on campus and promoting the Prime Student brand while educating students on the services provided. We were required to set up fun and engaging events for students. We were supplied with items to give to students and were required to reach a minimum of 300 students per event activation. We used social media platforms, including Instagram, Snapchat, and Twitter to promote our events.

Towards the end of my fall semester, I got the opportunity to do undergraduate research with my International Marketing professors. To top things off, I was trying to get good grades in my classes and build up my academic grade point average. This was the most stressful time in my life. I was averaging five hours of sleep, and I was at school for 14 hours of my day as a commuter student going to campus every day.

I nearly burned out several times throughout the year but managed to work through the stress and was able to achieve my goals. I was so focused on completing tasks that I didn't have time to think about how the stress was affecting my mind and body. Thankfully, I was able to push through the struggle, stress, and reached my goal. On May 5, 2018, I graduated Magna Cum Laude from Florida Atlantic University.

I looked back at my rollercoaster undergraduate experience and appreciated the path I took and the effort I put in. To achieve my goals although I had many obstacles in my path, I had to work meticulously, consumed plenty of caffeine, and had a positive mindset.

Furthermore, in looking back on my personal background, being from an immigrant household was challenging but very rewarding for me as well. I was born in the United States, so I had an advantage in growing up learning English, so there was not a struggle with a language or cultural barrier that my parents experienced.

My parents spoke Spanish at home, so I was blessed with being bilingual from an early age. I love being able to communicate with people in a different language and know that not everyone around us understood what we were saying. To me, it is like speaking in a different code, and I would automatically feel more connected to the person I am communicating with in Spanish.

Besides language, I grew up with an influence of both American and Latino cultures. I learned early in my life that not everyone around me spoke the same language at home, ate the same foods, celebrated the same holidays, listened to the same music, and learned the same values as I did. Being a part of the Latino population automatically gives an advantage in the Latin American community. It is a benefit to have a community within this country that shares a similar upbringing, language, and culture that differs from the mainstream America.

I believe assimilating into a country is important for immigrants because connecting to the new environment and culture opens their perspectives and helps them adapt to the American society. But it is also important to stay connected with one's cultural and ethnic roots because they are a big part of the immigrant's identity.

As I have gotten older, I have noticed there are different subgroups when it comes to immigrant families. The main subgroups I have seen are the following: foreign-born citizens, first-generation citizens, and second-generation citizens. Foreign-born citizens, like my parents, were raised in a completely different setting and had to adapt to the cultural differences later on in their lives in America. They experienced a different childhood and usually do not feel as comfortable assimilating with a new American culture. Foreign-born citizens are more connected to the culture they were born in.

My parents have lived in the United States for more years than they have in the Dominican Republic, but they feel more comfortable speaking Spanish than English and associating with the Dominican Republic culture. Foreign-born citizens are more likely to have an accent compared to first- or second-generation citizens. Foreign-born citizens generally have the strongest connection to their cultural roots. First generation citizens, like myself, have a different upbringing than foreign-born citizens.

I have been influenced by my Dominican Republic culture in my household and through my family, but I was also heavily influenced by the American culture that surrounds me. Since I live in America, the influence of American culture is far more influential in my up-bringing than my Dominican Republic culture is. My parents really pushed for my brother and me to be raised as Americans and adapt to the American culture because they did not want us to go through the same hardships they experienced as immigrants from the Dominican Republic.

However, my parents made sure we were raised connected to and proud of our Dominican Republican roots. I spent many summers of my youth in the Dominican Republic. It was interesting seeing the differences in the mindsets of the people from the Dominican Republic compared to America. When I would go to the Dominican Republic, at times, I felt like an outsider because I was seen as American instead of Dominican Republican. I wanted to fit in with the kids from the country of Dominical Republic that I take pride in being a part of but have been raised in such a different American culture that I automatically stand out from the people there in the Dominican Republic. This was more difficult for me growing up because, as a kid, I always wanted to fit in and find an identity for myself. As I got older, I realized I am not either, or, but both.

Lastly, I am excited about my future in America. I hope to be a marketing professional and to use my talents to assist my family and my community.

CHAPTER 13
"MICHELLE"
DIAMOND IN THE ROUGH

I was born and raised in Barranquilla, Colombia. I grew up with the platonic idea of one day visiting Disneyland and getting to know my favorite actors and actresses, but this idea seemed so far from reality that I decided to keep it in the back of my head along with other dreams. In fact, thanks to my brother and my sister, I grew up listening to a lot of music in English, like rock and techno.

At the beginning of fourth grade in Colombia, my school started a bilingual program, and we would all study English as a Second Language (ESL) courses, along with the rest of our academic curriculum. The learning all came to me so easily; I was quick to understand some concepts and to apply them as if nothing was new to me.

I started to watch TV with subtitles in English and to pay attention to the lyrics I listened to. All this helped me to improve my English abilities and comprehension. Further, I had the chance to go to bilingual education camps in my area to practice my skills and to meet native English speakers. I was given all these opportunities, and my English speaking skills kept on getting better. I knew I was far from speaking the English language perfectly, and visiting the United States or any other nation in which English was the primary language was beyond what my family could afford. To me, there were no second chances. I had to get it right. I did not see any travel opportunities to which I could apply my English language skills.

During those middle school years, my parents were constantly fighting over financial and money issues, and I was not doing well in school. Hence, I started to focus on what I wanted to do with my life. I looked into universities in my city, anything related to journalism, because that has always been what I wanted to do. I was waiting to graduate from school and finally begin my journey as a journalist. However, this did not happen the way I expected.

In December of 2014, the year of my sixteenth birthday, my parents had recently split up, and their separation hit me like a cold blizzard. My mother had decided to take a trip to the United States with the intention of getting away from my dad and the hope of finding herself again. She moved to New Jersey where one of her childhood friends lived. My mother's friend let my mother stay in her house, helped her find a part time job to feel productive, and it was then that she decided she would stay in the United States permanently.

During that time, my sister and I were living with my older brother and his family. It was hard to live far away from my mom for a couple of months. Yet, I had the hope she would come back to stay in Colombia. However, just two days into her visit, my mother told us that she had decided to stay in the United States for a long time.

I was the youngest of my siblings. My sister was finishing medical school, and my brother had started a family. It made sense for me to be the one to go with my mother. I left my friends, a great part of my family, and almost my entire life there in Colombia. However, it was worth it to come to the United States because I was finally with my mom again. After a long couple of months without seeing her, we started our new lives in the United States.

I went back to school, and my mother started to work in things she had never done before, such as cleaning houses, but she never gave up. She had always been an inspiration to me, but without a doubt, seeing her persevere through all her struggles gave me greater reason to be inspired.

I cannot deny the fact that for the first couple of weeks in America I was in shock. I was not able to enjoy New York City —or literally anything—because of the constant thought that my life had changed completely. I had moved into a new country and a new city. I was learning a new language in America. Until the day it hit me, I felt almost as if my mind had stopped functioning because of the cultural shock. Later, I realized that I had come to the United States to stay permanently.

Even though I had been taught English since I was nine years old, the language barrier was still there. The pace of speaking English I had learned was slightly different from the English most mainstream Americans would speak —mine was a lot slower.

It took me a couple of months and some English as a Second Language (ESL) classes to sharpen and speed up my speaking. Luckily, I started my junior year of high school in regular classes, which meant no more ESL classes. I felt as if I had been thrown into a deep pool, and, to this day, I do not know how to swim.

I wanted to do better in school, to prove I was up to the challenge. Honestly, it was trying at first and not exactly because of the English language barrier but because of my classmates. I remembered sitting in my English class; we had to sit in groups to read a poem and find the literary devices within the text. It was my turn to read, and there was a specific word I did not know how to pronounce. One of my classmates laughed in my face, and, from that day on, she acted as if I were inferior to her. That clashing against cultural expectations hurt my feelings, and I had to scramble to keep up eventually diminished my self-confidence.

In truth, once you come to a different country and try your best to adapt, some people will try to shut you down. It is like the tossing and tumbling in a jewelry tumbler. I have been studying English since the fourth grade. At this public school, classmates acted like I was less smart just because I pronounced certain words differently or did not yet know alternate meanings of words familiar to them. Experiences like that one made me feel bad about myself. To this day, I hate that I still speak with some Spanish accent in my English words.

In reflecting upon my positive experiences growing up as an immigrant youth in the United States, I have found some great success. I have accepted Jesus Christ as my Savior, and every day I strive to live a life according to God's will. I have gotten closer to my mother. I understand other cultures. I am finally following my dream of going to school for journalism and am pleased that my stories have been published in the college's newspaper.

I believe coming to the United States was not a coincidence, and it may not have been the most enjoyable experience at first. However, my growing up process in America surely built my character and helped me grow as the woman I am today. My immigrant experience has taught me that the story of every immigrant is not just how we got here, but about who we have become along the way, because even the most beautiful gems need to be polished. My life is in the process of being "polished" to be the best I can be in America. In the future, I hope to be a journalist to make a difference in my community.

CHAPTER 14
"JONATHAN G."
BEYOND THE BASICS

My family and I came to the United States on June 12, 2009. We are a family of five – my dad, mom, sister, brother, and me. When we arrived, I was about to turn 14 years old.

I was born and raised in El Salvador, the smallest country in Central America. When we came to the United States, neither my family nor I spoke English. Our extended family members already living here in America had most of what we needed such as beds, a TV, food, water, etc.

We had the support of our extended family members. My dad already had a job since we got our legalized paperwork though a company. But our family still struggled financially because my father was not earning enough money to pay for more than basic living necessities.

I was happy because I had always dreamed about coming to the United States, but the adjustment was more difficult than I imagined. My plan was to get a good education, so I could help my family. Those first years I was just a regular kid during the week, doing my home assignments and participating in school activities, but on the weekends

I worked. My brother and I did extra jobs with my dad and uncle to help bring in extra money.

Looking back, I would say the most difficult adjustment has been learning how to speak, write, and understand English. In school, I struggled the most. It was the uncertainty. I had long class periods and had to pay attention and try focusing on the topic being explained in a language I didn't understand. I had just five minutes to find my way to the next class, and since I didn't know much English, when I asked for directions, people could not understand my speaking words. Then there was lunch. I didn't know what food to point to, because even the American food was new to me.

My classes were supposed to be "easy," but because of my limited experience with the English language, even those classes challenged me. It was extremely difficult to do homework or any after school activity. I had to ask my cousins for help, and there were times that nobody was there to help me unravel my homework assignments, so I had to figure them out by myself. Those years were hard for me to adjust my life in America.

Being the first child in my family was not easy, either. I always tried to set a good example, to model the right way to behave, so that my brother and sister would follow in my footsteps, or at least see what was best for them. Parental expectations added more weight on me, being an immigrant youth. I felt the burden to become someone important in life. I knew that I was going to be the first in my family to accomplish lots of things, and I sometimes let those thoughts pressure me.

Furthermore, adapting to a new community and a new culture were very difficult for me as an immigrant youth from El Salvador. American schools and neighborhoods are totally different, and I was not sure what I was supposed to do to fit in. Sometimes I wondered if I would ever fit in, but I did not want to give up.

Although I experienced difficult times growing up as an immigrant youth from El Salvador, I am very grateful for having my parents and family with me in the United States. One of the most positive things about growing up in America was having my parents' total support. Even if they did not understand what was going on, my parents were still there with me. My high school teachers taught me what I needed to know about my high school environment, and they helped me make sense of the new experiences and create bridges connecting to my Salvadoran culture.

However, the most positive thing growing up as an immigrant youth in the United States was being qualified to attend the Enlightened Initiative (EI) camp in 2013. I learned many different leadership skills that to this date I am still using. We were encouraged to honor our heritage, culture, and faith teaching. Acknowledging that God is in my life, I now understand that He has a purpose for my life. I am so grateful for each and every person who has helped me to become the person I am today. I will always have them in my heart.

Before the EI camp, I used to be a very shy person and not really at ease with people. In school, I did what I was supposed to do, but I did not participate in class as much — that is, I did not step up.

During the EI camp, I learned so much about becoming a leader: how to work with a group and to communicate with people, how to do presentations, learn more about math and science, and even learned more English vocabulary words. I learned so much that it changed me and helped me look at things differently: beyond the basics.

After the EI camp, when I returned to my high school, I participated more with school activities and helped a club organized an International Night. For that event, we collected food and put on a talent show. With more confidence, I organized a group in my high school, and we went out to collect food for Manna Food Center, an organization that helps homeless people in Maryland.

I even joined the football team for my school, even though I did not know how to play that game. I helped students with their homework assignments during lunch hours. I participated in a program with the Smithsonian Institution with one of my teachers. I graduated with two scholarships, and I was an English as a Second Language student of the year for the Wheaton and Kensington Chamber of Commerce. I got a certificate awarded which was signed by Maryland State Senator Roger Manno.

The Enlightened Initiative (EI) camp really helped me become who I am now and not be so fearful of taking chances. Now, I have graduated from a community college with an Associate degree in Criminal Justice, and I am currently working in an immigration law firm. I hope one day that I can become a police officer. I have exceeded my early expectations, have begun to fulfill my dreams, and am committed to support and guide others to get beyond the basics, too.

CHAPTER 15
"JULIE"
ADVANTAGES OF ADVERSITY

W e separated in order to live as a family. This sounds a little strange, but when you know my story, you will understand. My parents immigrated to the United States from El Salvador. They met and lived in California because it was easier to blend into the Latino community there. For several years, my parents lived below the radar, illegally, but they worked hard and eventually obtained their green cards, becoming residents to remain in this country legally. The first of their seven children were born there. It was not until they moved all the way across the continent to Virginia that my other sister, brother, and I were born. We became a family of seven.

My childhood was going great until devastating financial problems tore our family apart. First, we lost our home. This led to bad credit. Bad credit made it impossible for my parents to get another house. It was impossible to find a decent, affordable apartment large enough for us all. No landlord was willing to allow seven people to live on their property, especially a family of immigrants. Everywhere we went, landlords turned us away, intimidated by our Central American culture and the size of our family. We had to split up.

Those years, living apart from other family members, led to dangerous but enlightening experiences. My parents taught us to be where we were supposed to be every day and on time. At thirteen years of age, I was homeless. I was sleeping on the ramp at my old elementary school, so that I would not be late to school.

Later, fortunately, my parents were able to save money to find lodging for the whole family. We had moved south to Woodbridge, Virginia, and we commuted north to Springfield, Virginia five days a week for school. We did not switch schools because we had better opportunities in the schools located in Springfield. My parents worked hard to assure that we got the best education available.

Not surprisingly, the family struggled just to stay afloat. Succumbing to the anguish and stress due to finances, some family members sought escape and became substance abusers. It was very frustrating; they were working hard to do the right thing, and then to have doors slammed in their faces just because they were immigrants from a Central American country of El Salvador. It was exasperating striving to support the family on the limited employment opportunities. The financial stress was getting them down. Some floated on the highs of illicit drugs.

However, just a few years later, things turned around for us. We found a basement to rent. Though our family had financial troubles, we usually lived in neighborhoods populated with immigrant Spanish speakers like us. I was comfortable at school because many students around me were from Latin American backgrounds, too. Our family eventually worked its way up to getting an apartment where all seven of us could live together again.

Looking back, I see that despite the difficult times of being homeless and living away from some family members, growing up as an immigrant youth teaches valuable lessons. My personal experiences have instilled a level of diversity awareness that serves me well today. I know better than to judge others based on their cultures or beliefs.

I now recognize the positive aspects of my childhood experiences. I can speak, read, and write English and Spanish. This will make me more competitive in the workplace when I am ready to enter the job market. I am also blessed that my mother was able to find many programs for Latinos/as, as that helped us get food, clothes, and other things to survive. I can lead others to what I have learned, modeling that hard working El Salvadorian immigrants can succeed in the United States.

Furthermore, in reflecting back on my life, being an immigrant youth is a blessing. My parents migrated here to give my siblings and me an opportunity to live, learn, and lead. Not everyone here gets to experience programs like the summer camp sponsored by the Enlightened Initiative (EI). It was designed especially for youth just like me, who are immigrant and refugee youth that come from low-wealth backgrounds. While I know as an immigrant youth that I do not live in privilege in America, I am grateful for opportunities that support my growth and leadership as an immigrant youth in the United States because of non-profits and programs that believe in the promises of success for refugee and immigrant youth.

Fortunately, I will not let my difficult family issues divert me from becoming the best person I can be. I have learned that there are some advantages to going through adversity. We have become resourceful and have learned to cope. I am more resilient now. I am reminded of this attitude about living that advises avoiding people not committed to your success. Moreover, we should not allow stereotypes or nasty words to get to us. Instead, we should prove naysayers wrong! We learn to hope and to work hard. We become resilient, learning how to get back up and keep going to reach our dreams.

That's my goal! What else can I do, surrounded by family who fought for years to keep us together, supported by friends who cheer me on, and loved by parents who did not give up since immigrating from El Salvador? It is their modeling that spurs me to maximize opportunities to get a good education. It is my goal to make them proud by getting good grades in school, maintaining perfect attendance, and participating in programs such as the Enlightened Initiative and school service clubs to develop and demonstrate my leadership abilities and expand my potential as a servant leader.

CHAPTER 16
"HONG"
METAMORPHOSIS OF
A DOUBLE ADOPTEE

She smelled different. Not better, not worse, just different. Even these many years later, that olfactory memory floats through my mind when I recall what my Chinese adopted mother told me about the day she got me — or, more precisely, the day my biological mother gave me to the lady who first adopted me.

He looked at me funny. Whenever we two were alone, my older brother gave me shredding looks like he did not really like me, like he wanted to cut me out of their life. He was fifteen years old and knew the law. I did not realize until years later that he probably was jealous of me because my adoptive Chinese mother paid more attention to me than to him, her first child and a legal citizen.

You see, back in China when I was born, a family was allowed to have only one child. Additional children were considered illegal. However, if a family were to have an additional child, that Chinese family had to pay almost ⊠80000 ($13,000 American dollars) to the Chinese government as a penalty for having another child in the family. Although the laws began changing in 2016, back then I was both illegal and costly in that single parent family.

How did I come to be a part of a Chinese family that already had a teenage son? Here's what I learned.

The Egg

In the winter of 2003, a middle-aged woman is going out of town on a trip. While she waits for the bus, she notices a tired young woman holding an agitated baby. The baby is wriggly and restless, and the young lady looks exhausted. She looks over to the older lady and asks, "Can you hold my baby for me while I go to the bathroom?"

"Sure, why not?" replies the older lady, recalling how worn out she had felt years before when her own son had been wiggly and weepy like that. "Sure, take your time. I'll be right here. My bus won't arrive for another forty-five minutes or so." She cradles the baby against her ample bosom and hums one of her son's favorite songs. The young mother seems surprised and relieved that the baby settles so quickly in the arms of another woman. She glances back, then walks briskly to the bathroom.

The middle-aged woman's bus comes, but the baby's mother has not returned. The middle-aged woman goes to the bathroom to check to see if the young woman is there. She is not in the bathroom, nor has she returned to the place the two women had been sitting earlier.

The older woman waits and walks, trying to calm the now wailing infant and avoid the strange looks of other passengers, obviously annoyed by her inability to quiet the child. She misses a lot of buses that night. It is getting late, and the young woman still does not come back. The middle-aged woman realizes the infant will need to have her dirty diaper changed and to get something to eat, so she takes the baby home.

The next morning, she returns to the bus station, certain the young mother will be anxious to know what happened to her child. But the mother is not there that day or the next two days. The older woman finally realizes that this young mother will not be coming back to get her little baby.

No one tells the middle-aged woman what to do; she's single and does not have to consult with a husband; she simply thinks that the baby girl is a gift. Hence, she takes her home, gives her a name, and raises her as her own. She excitedly tells her 15-year-old son that he now has his own baby sister.

The Caterpillar

I, of course, am that baby girl now living with the single woman and her son. I was ten years old when I heard that story and learned that I was not only an adopted child, I was also an abandoned baby. None of this was likely to come out if my adoptive mother had not gone to the Public Security Bureau to seek the help of the media to find funds for me to get further education.

It may have been during these conversations that I learned that my biological parents had divorced a few months before I was born and that my biological father had become ill and died a few months later. But there were other issues for the single woman who had adopted and cared for me the first ten years of my life.

In China, I did not attend a public school because my family could not afford to pay the fees. Furthermore, I was considered what Chinese society would call an "Heihaizi." This is the definition I found on Wikipedia: (Chinese: pinyin: hēiháizi) or a "black child" is a term applied in China. A Heihaizi refers to children born outside of the Chinese government's One-Child Policy or generally Chinese children who are not registered in the national household registration system.

It was very expensive for my single, adoptive Chinese mom to care for me, but she did not abandon me like my biological mom had done. By the time I was ten years old, my Chinese mother believed that I should not have to live as an "Heihaizi" all my life. As a "Heihaizi," I could only attend elementary school years and would not be allowed to attend secondary school. Hence, in the unforgettable summer of 2015, my mother sought ways to help me become a legal citizen of China.

My mom's sister said that she had a great idea – get a news media reporter to help me! My aunt had heard of a story of an impoverished girl who wanted to attend college. She called the local television sta tion and told the reporter that her mother would not allow her to go to college. The reporter's heart went out to the girl, and she arranged an interview. From the start, the reporters saw it as a "scam", but thought it would be a good story to tell about a girl was not being permitted to further her education. The news reporting attracted good hearted people and enough stepped up to help the girl attend a college.

My aunt tried to do the same thing for me by asking a news re-porter to interview me. But that didn't work. The news report was not enough to convince the local Chinese neighborhood committee, primarily because we did not have the proper official birth documents to help me become a Chinese citizen. So, we had to go to a different plan through the Public Security Bureau who eventually issued me a certificate of an abandoned baby, which, in turn, qualified me to be-come a resident of the local children's welfare home.

A few days later, the police took us to the Guiyang Children's Welfare Institute (CWI). It was not as cruel as it sounds. There was a reason for all of this. By going to the CWI, I became eligible for government assistance through a program that helps abandoned babies or orphans become citizens of China. But if I were to live in the chil-dren's welfare home, I could no longer live with my Chinese adoptive mom, and she would no longer be my legal guardian. We both were very sad, but also knew it was the best route to my becoming a citizen of China.

Living in the Children's Welfare Institute (CWI), I shared a large bedroom with five other residents. The primary adult in my life be-came a teacher, not my mother. Fortunately, because my situation was quite special, the leaders of the children's welfare home allowed my adoptive mother to take me home during the holiday seasons, but I always had to return to the CWI afterwards.

Then, the next year, when I was eleven years old, the dean of the CWI sought me out. She asked if I wanted to go to the United States in the summer for two weeks. At that time, all I really knew about the United States was that it was a country mentioned on national Chinese television and that America is the home of the Kentucky Fried Chicken. I never imagined I would ever go there.

This was a happy and sad time. It was exciting to imagine myself in the United States, but scary to think I might never see my Chinese family again. I had heard rumors I might be adopted by an American family, so you can imagine my relief when the CWI dean assured me it was just a two-week summer camp. When I called my adoptive mother that night, she was as surprised and happy as I was. Her reaction helped me relax a bit and agree to go on the adventure.

Throughout the summer, I had a good time with the other eight children who went with me for two weeks of camp in the United States. Still, it was great to return to China. That fall, I became a seventh grader. My attention was all on the new school's activities, teachers, and meeting new friends. Time flew by the three years I lived at CWI, from the 5th to 8th grade, plus I grew from 147 centimeters to 157 centimeters.

Then, at the end of 2016, I began hearing buzz around Children's Welfare Institute that I might be adopted by the Americans. A few months later, the CWI dean confirmed that rumor. It turned out that the American family who fostered me that year of summer camp wanted to adopt me. I would become a member of their family. This confused me. I was already adopted. I already had a family. What was going on?

When I called my Chinese adoptive mother, I sensed her feelings were as scrambled as mine. She was middle-aged when I came to her.

This was over a decade later. At first, she did not want me to go, but later she told me I should go to the United States where there would be more opportunities. She was a single mom. In the United States, I would have both a mom and dad who would love me. Reluctantly, I conceded. It was with equally mixed feelings that I spent that the last Chinese New Year with my adoptive Chinese family while the adoption papers were being prepared.

The Chrysalis

My American parents adopted me when I was 13 years and 11 months old. They enrolled me right away in their middle school with just three months left of the semester. It was rough, and I resisted. Even though in China from the third grade students are taught English, I didn't like it and paid little attention to the English lessons. After six years of schooling there, I only remembered the 26 letters of the alphabet and the most basic greetings in English. I never really believed I would have to speak English to English speakers!

At first, my second adoptive parents here in the United States had to use Google translate to communicate with me. The tension built, and I struggled to learn the new language and understand the strange culture. I spun a shell around myself. After school, I would come home, hide in my room, and video chat with my friends in China. I played with my cell phone until late in the evening thinking that would help make me relax. Cocooning in my room was a simple escape from the cultural shock of living in the United States.

By going to school, I was exhausted by the school's activities. I hid in my room at home and did not take any initiative to make friends at school. My American parents would knock on the door, inquiring about my health and telling me to come down to dinner. Impatiently and impolitely, I would declare, "I'm not hungry!" Then I would stop talking. The new language and the American culture scared me.

However, there were still many students in the school who were very friendly to me and tried to help me often. It might be because of the students' goodwill or my own awakening that I needed to make friends. That summer, it finally dawned on me that this was not how I wanted to live my life in the United States. I did not like the person I was becoming. If I wanted to be different, I would have to make an effort, learn to talk articulately, accept the overtures, and make new friends.

The Butterfly

High school proved to be a new environment and a new beginning. I decided to change. I stopped avoiding people, afraid that they might laugh at me because my English was not good. Because I began to extend myself, students started to listen more attentively to my "Chinglish." Of course, because of my pronunciation, some people who did not understand my accented English still chose to ignore me.

Fortunately, some students and adults in my high school extended their friendship. As I paid attention to my classmates' patience, I became more assertive about asking questions. They generously took time to clarify what I didn't understand. I began to try new things, be more cheerful, and even try out for a new sport in my high school. I emerged from my shell, talking more with my adoptive American parents and exploring new options for an immigrant teenager in the United States.

I know that these special experiences are only a small part of my life. There will be more challenges and changes in the future. I would imagine, at the end of the story, I will laugh at these experiences. I know now that I truly am grateful. I have had three moms who only wanted the best for me — my biological mom who gave me to someone she thought could take better care of me; my adoptive Chinese mom who as a single mom raised me for ten years, then sought ways for me to get the official papers leading to legal status as a Chinese citizen and qualifying me for a second adoption, this time by two parents in the United States. I am a double adoptee who has been triply blessed!

CHAPTER 17
AFTERWORD

In writing my own refugee story and the stories of the other immigrant youth, I am humbled and honored to know these amazing young people who are now living in the United States.

Because of these young immigrants and refugees, I have shared my own personal refugee story. Additionally, I have dedicated this book to share their courage, resilience, commitment, hardships, obstacles, hard work, perseverance, patience, determination, and love for their families, friends, and communities and for the broader American society.

By writing this book, they have shared with me these important themes.

First of all, these young immigrants work very hard to survive and to be accepted into the American mainstream society. They are willing to work part-time after school and on weekends to earn money in order to help their parents pay bills and survive in this American society. They are wearing two "shirts" – meaning that they have a life outside of their cultural ethnic homes where they speak English and want to fit into the American society, and they also have a life inside their cultural ethnic homes where they need to be respectful and deferential to their parents and older siblings and not to be too "vocal" inside their home.

Second, the immigrant youth know that they come from low-wealth backgrounds, so they must work part-time jobs along with going to school full-time to survive in their communities and neighborhoods. They see how their parents survive and how their parents work very hard to put food on the table for the whole family to eat. They know that they must work to help pay the household bills.

Third, the immigrant youth value education; they see education as a pathway to get out of poverty and an opportunity to have a career to obtain the "American Dream" for themselves and for their families. They are willing to study late into the night after coming home from working part-time to pay the household bills. Plus, some youth see their weekends as opportunities to catch up on their school projects and homework activities.

Fourth, the immigrant youth want to be leaders of their communities and schools. They want to lead through community service and through volunteerism to promote civic duties in their neighborhoods. Sometimes, they do not see role models in the media who look like they do. They are hungry to see leaders and role models who do look like them because they also want to give back and to serve their schools and communities.

Fifth, the immigrant youth appreciate the American culture and want to learn the English language. They see learning the American culture as a wonderful experience in their lives. While growing up in America has been a tough struggle, they like the American culture and see the positive sides of what this culture offers. However, they still love their own ethnic cultures, traditions, languages, and food as well. Given that the young immigrants are open to try new things, they appreciate the American culture, and they want to learn the English language.

Sixth, the immigrant youth know that they will encounter significant hardships and obstacles to grow up in America, but they believe in themselves, and they want to go after their dreams and not give up. Many of these young immigrants are quite resilient.

Seventh, the youth have a strong connection with their faith and religion. For some, Jesus Christ, as God in their lives, has helped them to deal with the very difficult and tough times in their lives as immigrant and refugee youth in the United States. Because of God's crucible of severe trials and the fiery tests of leaving their native countries and resettling into America, the young immigrants have become aware of who they are in their new homeland.

While some people in the federal, state, or local governments or in other organizations and institutions do not understand the circumstances and lives of the immigrant and refugee youth and their families, I want to share how they are just like you and me in this wonderful nation called the United States of America. That is, the young immigrants and refugees want to be the best that they can be in terms of obtaining the best education, housing, healthcare, and careers to provide for their families and to give back to their communities, and eventually to the American society.

While we still in our current times encounter racism, prejudice, negative stereotypes, and unconscious bias against the immigrant youth and their families, this book aims to educate and to share how beautifully the youth have worked to make America a "beacon of hope" to everyone around the world.

Many youth have expressed to me that by living in the United States, they have realized the potential to reach their dreams of working as doctors, engineers, business leaders, politicians, pastors, lawyers, police officers, teachers, marine biologists, marketers, and entrepreneurs in this wonderful nation.

Additionally, many of these youth will become our future leaders, and we must continue to nurture, support, encourage, and invest in them as their generation leads this complex nation into the next decade and beyond. As a caring and generous nation, we cannot afford to lose the youth and their valuable contributions acquired by all they have undergone, suffered, and triumphed over to come here and join the American experience.

The United States has always been a country of immigrants and refugees. In 2012, children of immigrant parents accounted for one out of four children (25%), for a total of 18.4 million youth. Nearly six in ten children with immigrant parents have a parent who is an American citizen, and nearly all children in immigrant families (89%) are themselves United States citizens. In 2050, there will be at least 33 million immigrant youth in the nation. Plus, by 2050, America will be filled with so many diverse cultures and ethnic groups to comprise this great nation.

There are more than 11.5 million undocumented immigrants, 1.7 million of whom are Asian American, living in the United States. The top five countries of origin for Asian American undocumented individuals are India, China, South Korea, the Philippines, and Vietnam.

Moreover, I would like to share with you an additional spiritual perspective on the refugee and immigrant youth and their families who come to the United States. A Christian intercessor who has been praying for this book was awakened in the middle of the night and sensed the following impressions from God while in prayer:

"Many people are coming to this land, this land that I formed with a destiny planned before the foundations of the world. I fashioned this land with My own hands for a dream, a plan of My own, a plan to contain My light, the light of My glory, a light that would beckon and draw those people I would call to fill this place from every tribe and tongue and nation to represent My kingdom here on earth. The liberty they see here, even from a distance, is the true liberty of My Spirit, which sets all men *free*.

These I have called here are My jewels, forged in the fires of My crucible, enduring many hardships, trials, and tribulations, and dreaming of a better life . . . a life I have called them to in a new land where they can fulfill the plans I have ordained for them and for you *together* before the foundations of the world."

> *"If you do away with the yoke of oppression, with the pointing finger and malicious talk, and if you spend yourselves in behalf of the hungry and satisfy the needs of the oppressed, then your light will rise in darkness, and your night will become like the noonday. The Lord will guide you always; he will satisfy your needs in a sun-scorched land and will strengthen your frame. You will be like a well-watered garden, like a spring whose waters never fail. Your people will rebuild the ancient ruins and will raise up the age-old foundations; you will be called Repairer of Broken Walls, Restorer of Streets with Dwellings."* (Isaiah 58:9-12 New International Version)

Lastly, I want to express my call of action on behalf of the refugee and immigrant youth and their families. As a caring and prosperous nation, we need to invest in the immigrant and refugee youth in their neighborhoods, in their urban and rural communities, and in their schools across this beautiful and complex nation. This is because these vulnerable youth have the potential to become our leaders, and they are worth the support and investment from all of us. For example, we need to increase educational and academic scholarship opportunities, improve healthcare and housing access, and expand job opportunities for the youth and their families. We must mentor them and guide them as the future leaders that this country desperately needs. The immigrant youth strengthen us with their valuable contributions. The youth are our future, and we must invest in them in order to sustain the beauty of the diversity of cultures, the growing economic expansion, and the politics of inclusion in this amazing nation.

The Enlightened Initiative's mission is to empower immigrant and vulnerable youth from low-wealth backgrounds by building their leadership skills, increasing their cultural competence and mental wellness, expanding their math and science knowledge and interest, developing their communication skills and fostering sincere friendships that would be lasting and beneficial to the immigrant youth, their families, schools, and their communities.

How you can partner with us...

Visit http://enlightenedinitiative.org/leadershipcamp/

- Provide scholarships for some refugee and immigrant youth to attend the summer leadership camp in Washington, D.C. for youth from the 8th grade to the 12th grade.

- Book Mr. Cuong as a keynote speaker on leadership on refugee and immigrant youth and families, or for leadership workshops and sessions on leadership development and cultural sensitivity to work with refugee and immigrant youth across the nation.

- Host a day or half-day leadership development and cultural sensitivity sessions and workshops. Please contact Mr. Huynh directly at 301-273-5866 or cuongh14@gmail.com.

ABOUT THE AUTHOR

Mr. Cuong Quy Huynh is the author of his book, God's Crucible: We Who Dream of a Better Life – Stories of Hope by Refugee and Immigrant Youth. Mr. Huynh is a former WK Kellogg Foundation Fellow (2014-2016). He is also the President and Founder of a non-profit organization, Enlightened Initiative (EI), to serve vulnerable refugee and immigrant youth from low-wealth communities and families across the nation and Puerto Rico. He was a Fellow with the America's Leaders of Change Program sponsored by the National Urban Fellows in 2012.

Mr. Huynh was also a senior policy and program analyst for the National Aeronautics and Space Administration (NASA) where he started as a Presidential Management Fellow. He has analyzed over twenty-five Earth and space science programs totaling in excess of $600 million. Mr. Huynh graduated with a law degree from University of California, Hastings College of the Law as a Thurgood Marshall Fellow. He also graduated with a master's degree in public policy from The University of Chicago as a Woodrow Wilson Fellow.

a Book's Mind

Whether you want to purchase bulk copies of
God's Crucible
or buy another book for a friend, get it now at:
www.abooksmart.com

If you have a book that you would like to publish,
contact Jon McHatton, Publisher, at A Book's Mind:
info@abooksmind.com.

www.abooksmind.com

73877714R00064

Made in the
USA
Middletown, DE